PAINTING AND LINING

TO JENNY

Designed by Paul Karau
Printed by Amadeus Press, Cleckheaton

Published by
WILD SWAN PUBLICATIONS LTD.
1-3 Hagbourne Road, Didcot, Oxon, OX11 8DP

A MODELLER'S HANDBOOK OF
PAINTING AND LINING

by
Ian Rathbone

WILD SWAN PUBLICATIONS

FOREWORD

A good model has to be dimensionally accurate, operate well, be put together properly and be well painted. There may be other attributes the individual requires in his perception of the 'good model' but I think that the above four are the most important. As a professional painter of models I always look at the paintwork first and if that passes my critical eye I then consider the rest of it. It is true that an average model can be enhanced by excellent paintwork but an excellent model can be destroyed by poor painting

CONTENTS

INTRODUCTION 1

CHAPTER ONE – BEFORE STARTING 3

CHAPTER TWO – PREPARATION 11

CHAPTER THREE – PRIMING 17

CHAPTER FOUR – PAINTING 21
    PAINTING METHODS 27
    AIRBRUSHING THE MODEL 31
    SPRAYING ENAMELS 35
    SPRAYING CELLULOSE 35
    SPRAYING ACRYLIC 37
    PAINTING WHEELS 37
    PAINTING THE CHASSIS 37
    MASKING 38
    FRISKET FILM 42

CHAPTER FIVE – LINING LOCOMOTIVES 55
    CORRECTING LINING ERRORS 55
    DRAWING CURVES 57
    INCURVED CORNERS 60
    MIXED TRAFFIC LINING 74
    ORDER OF LINING 76
    LMS CRIMSON LAKE ENGINES 1923-1936 WITH 'STRAW' LINING 79
    LMS CRIMSON LAKE ENGINES 1937-1939 WITH YELLOW LINING 82
    SOME PRE-GROUPING LIVERIES 84
    GWR/BR GREEN LOCOMOTIVE LINING 86
    LINING WHEELS 89
    GREAT WESTERN RAILWAY DOUBLE LINING STYLE 91

CHAPTER SIX – HAND LETTERING AND NUMBERING 99
    MAKING TRANSFERS 105
    WASP STRIPES 107

CHAPTER SEVEN – COACHES 109
    TEAK AND WOOD FINISHES 123
    COACH INTERIORS 128

CHAPTER EIGHT – WAGONS 130

CHAPTER NINE – READY-TO-RUN MODELS 133

CHAPTER TEN – RESTORATION 137
    PAINTING WOODEN BODIES 140

CHAPTER ELEVEN – FINISHING 141
    TRANSFERS 141
    NAME AND NUMBER PLATES 145
    VARNISHING 147

CHAPTER TWELVE – WEATHERING 149

APPENDIX
    SCALE WIDTHS OF LINING IN MILLIMETRES 152
    BRITISH RAILWAYS GREEN LOCOMOTIVE LINING 153
    BRITISH RAILWAYS AND LNWR BLACK LOCOMOTIVE LINING 153
    SUPPLIERS 154

This was my first real attempt at a 'proper' paint job. I built Papyrus in 1978 from a Wills kit. The kit was designed to be fitted to a Triang/Hornby Britannia chassis, but its first chassis was one milled out of solid brass bar by Steve Barnfield. I subsequently decided that I preferred compensation, so she now sits on my own scratchbuilt EM gauge frames with beam compensation. The valve gear is a dinosaur etch from Jamieson. She was painted using a basic Badger external-mix paint spray that cost me £4.99, powered by a spare tyre, and sprayed in the kitchen PP LNER Green and H satin black, with lettering by PC (now HMRS) Methfix transfers. The lining was done with a bow pen with home-made transfers for the splashers. The front of the cab is not lined – I didn't know how to then.

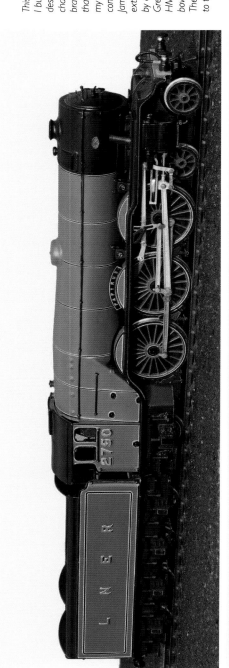

INTRODUCTION

I took up the hobby again (after marriage and children) in the mid 70s. The first locomotive kit that I built was a K's GWR Bulldog, stuck together with Araldite and painted with a friend's airbrush in Humbrol BR green. I thought it would look nice with some lining so I bought a sheet of Kemco waterslide GWR lining. With this I was able to line the engine, but the curves on the sheet wouldn't do the coal plate of the tender, so for that, I used a sheet of Kingsprint rub-down lining.

I was working in Peterborough at the time and lived near Bourne so when I had finished the engine I took it along to the Market Deeping MRC. Trouble was, there I met Steve Barnfield, who was already painting on a professional basis and doing all his lining with a draughtman's bow pen. My Bulldog didn't seem so good then.

The following weekend I went into the loft and found my drawing instruments that I had used as a student. I tried out the pens with paint and found that it worked well, so I have used a bow pen for lining ever since.

I have been building and painting model railway loco-motives and stock for nearly thirty years now, the last twelve as a professional. During that time I have continually updated the methods I use, either from experience or learning from others. I have been invited to demonstrate at most of the major exhibitions and to give talks to clubs and societies where I pass on the 'knowledge', but go away from each occasion having learnt something new myself.

I hope that this book will help you on your way; even if you don't master the bow pen for fine lining, there is much in here to help you to achieve a good basic finish, whatever the livery you choose.

What can we do to ensure that our model gets the painting it deserves? There are some basic ground rules, a lot of common sense, and the odd fudge. You may not be attempting Wainwright's Class D in the full glory of his South Eastern & Chatham livery or an ornate nineteenth century Great Western coach, but even a simple black engine deserves a fine smooth paint finish, even if it is to be weathered. Too often weathering is used to cover poor paintwork – and it shows. Many model makers can produce a well constructed model but then go on to ruin it with a poor paint job. I don't know why. If you've had the patience to do the research, learn construction techniques and spend many hours constructing the model, then the simple task of putting on a smooth coat of paint should not be beyond you.

Putting on the basic paintwork is a skill that all can learn. Lining is not a black art, it is not even an art; it is draughts-manship and, therefore, can also be learnt.

Although the book starts on the assumption that a kit is being built, the principles apply to the repainting of ready-to-run models. The book covers locomotives and coaches but the methods apply equally to wagons, trams, buses and other vehicles.

Paint references in the text prefixed P refer to Phoenix Precision and those prefixed H refer to the Humbrol range.

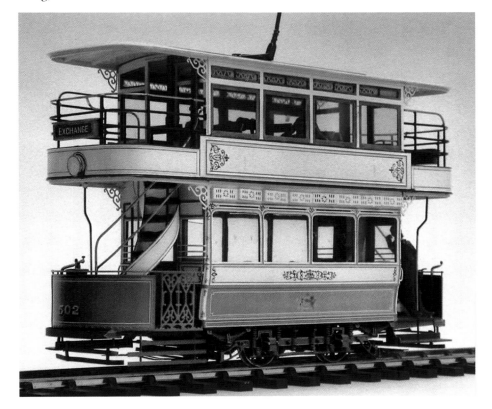

The origins of this 7mm scale etched brass kit are obscure, possibly it was a trial etch of a kit that was not marketed. The kit was built by Mike Edge. It was the first 7mm tram that I painted, and it was certainly a baptism of fire. As you can see, there is an awful lot of detail on a tram and a lot of fancy painting, both outside and in. The number on the dash panel is from the Methfix sheet 24 and the destination was cobbled together using the Microsoft 'Paint' program, on my, then, newly acquired PC. TONY WRIGHT

The Hornby-Dublo Standard Class 4 2-6-4T body was at the leading edge of RTR when introduced. Most of the mechanisms went under the Wills Stanier 2-6-4T, so the bodies are readily available at swapmeets. The body shape offers plenty of challenges for practising spraying on an even coat of paint, especially around the lubricators in front of the tanks. The shape of the tanks and back of bunker will also tax your lining skills, should you rise to the challenge.

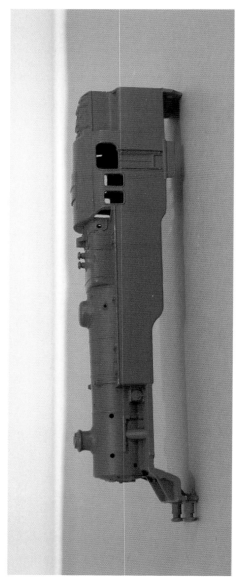

Hornby-Dublo tinplate coaches are excellent for practising painting coach liveries onto. They have very little value and can be stripped and painted as often as you like.

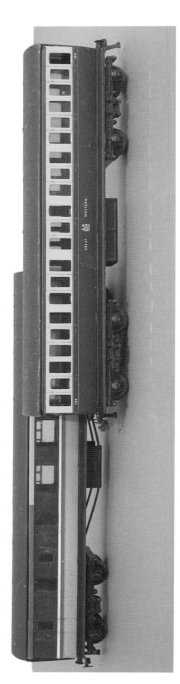

The other side of the two HD coaches. The corridor coach has been painted as a BR Intercity Buffet car, indicated by the red stripe over the 'kitchen' end. I painted this many years ago and the varnish is Floquil 'Flat Finish'. Unfortunately Flat Finish is quite waxy and can easily be scraped off with a finger nail or by packing and repacking at exhibitions. The suburban coach is painted in GWR Hawksworth style but is lacking the maroon droplights.

CHAPTER ONE
BEFORE STARTING

There are a number of things to do and take account of before applying paint. Painting your model is the last thing, the very last thing you should do.

PRACTICE

All the techniques for painting and lining that I describe require practice.

Get yourself an old body shell – preferably cast metal – for example, one of the old Hornby Dublo locomotives or coaches, which can often be found at swap-meets, for a few pounds. Alternatively, that first attempt at soldering a kit together, which didn't turn out quite as you would have liked. Your practice piece needs to be something that can be readily stripped of paint without damage to its surface. The Hornby Dublo locomotive castings, made of Mazak, can be painted and stripped ad infinitum, until you get your techniques sorted out. Likewise, the old pattern of coaches, made of tinplate, present a nice smooth surface for practising basic lining techniques. Basic spraying techniques can be practised on tin cans or any smooth material.

Even I have to practise. Although I am finishing models on a daily basis I may go some time without using a particular technique, usually because I am building a kit as well as painting it, so I practise it before resuming.

PATIENCE & PERSEVERANCE

This you will need in abundance. It is needed in two areas. Firstly having the perseverance to keep practising until you've got the techniques right before you apply it to your model. Then secondly, having the patience to wait for the paint to thoroughly dry and harden before you progress to the next stage. Lining, in particular, is a slow process – only one colour per side per day, or sometimes longer. This is very important.

PLANNING

Imagine you have just opened the box with a view to making a start and have just switched the soldering iron on. This is the first call on patience. Switch the iron off for a bit while you plan ahead.

If the engine has a lined livery, are there any parts of the completed model that will be particularly difficult to line out; for example, the cab front? I find that the back of the tender, some buffer beams and the front of cabs and side tanks are the worst to line out because of the bits and pieces that get in the way. Lamp brackets, vacuum pipes, buffers, couplings, safety valves, etc, could, in theory, be left off until after lining.

If you propose using cellulose paints you would do well to consider building up the model so that the sub-assemblies are a single colour.

If your model has lining on the curves of the splashers, cab sides or cab fronts it is much easier to make templates NOW while the parts are flat pieces of brass or white metal.

Does the tender have springs and axle boxes that are a different colour from the frames? Don't attach them until the painting is complete. In fact, even if they are the same colour, painting the frames, especially the little gap between spring and footplate, can be simplified by leaving the springs off.

Can you make up the model so that the boiler/smokebox/cab can be painted separately? It will make painting the footplate so much easier and cut out risky masking. This is very important if you propose to use cellulose paints.

If your model has number or name plates to be attached after painting, check that there are no rivets in those positions that will prevent the plate from sitting flat. Rivet counters have not yet developed the technology to detect missing rivets under plates, so file them off or don't press them out.

CONSTRUCTION

From a painter's point of view, essential tools during kit assembly are the setsquare or engineers' square and the straight edge. Lining on the model has to be straight and square, but also has to run parallel to the adjacent edge, but if the model itself is not straight and square you have an insoluble problem.

In my early days I once painted a locomotive whose cab was at a slight angle to the boiler, not readily apparent while it was unpainted. The livery was to be BR lined black. Having cleaned, primed and painted it and also part lined the tender, I had invested a fair bit of time in it so had to continue. When I had finished the lining on the cab sides, the lining, which is fairly bright, emphasised the lean on the cab and made the whole thing look a great deal worse. It is possible to compensate a little by putting on the lining square to a horizontal datum but then it is not parallel to the edges.

If you are building an etched kit, all the edges of the parts will have a double curve 'etching cusp' on them, together with the remains of one or more tabs. All exposed edges must have the cusps filed flat to remove the tab remains and improve the look of the finished product. It looks so much more professional if all the edges are clean and square – and it helps the painting too. A note here to etched kit designers – avoid putting tabs on the lower edge of valances and also on concave curves.

Whitemetal models generally show edges that are well over scale thickness. It is possible to file a bevel on visible edges so that they present a more scale appearance and, of course, the filing is so much easier if done before assembly.

There is a similar problem on some plastic models although recent products, helped by the fact that these are now perceived as scale models rather than toys, have commendably slim edges.

If the model has lining on the boiler bands I would recommend strongly that the boiler bands be left off the model; real-life boiler bands are simply strips of steel, typically about 2in wide by 3/32in or less, thick, and are there to hold the boiler cladding in position. In 0 gauge the scale thickness is about 0.002in and in 00, 0.001in. If the boiler cladding is etched in 18 thou material (as in 0 gauge), half etching gives a thickness of 9 thou, which is four and a half times too thick for the boiler bands. Whitemetal bands can be filed off, with care; separately etched bands can be left in the box. Etched-in boiler bands are harder to deal with, so you may just have to live with them.

Boiler bands on plastic models tend to be rather thick and could be made visually more acceptable by gentle filing down. Older plastic models have boiler bands that are semicircular in cross section (to enable lining with a brush in the factory). These certainly need attention, as it will be virtually impossible to get a transfer to lie on such a shape.

LNER 502. Although this is one of the usual three-quarter front view photographs taken in their millions, it gives a lot of clues to the livery of the period if it is examined carefully. The photo is not dated, but as the engine received its new LNER number in May 1946 and its BR number in July 1948, it can be narrowed down somewhat. Furthermore, there is a Route Availability number on the cab side, a feature introduced in September 1947, which narrows it still further. The photo has also been taken with film that could register red so that the lining on the black parts of the engine can be seen. The front frame extensions are lined on the outside but not the inside. The valance lining turns up behind the buffer beam. The cab front lining runs very close to the edge in order to run outside the spectacle frames. The cab side lining has curved corners, unlike a Doncaster engine. There is lining around the works plates, again not Doncaster practice. What the photo does not show us is the lining detail, if any, on the rear locomotive frames and the tender frames.

Does the prototype have unpainted steel hand rails? If so, assign the brass or nickel wire to the spares box and get some steel wire – nothing looks more like steel than steel. Alternatively, chemically blacken them. When you need to fit the boiler hand rails, bend them up but do not fix them – leave them until after .painting. If your model has painted hand rails, it is worthwhile chemically blackening them before painting so that future chips are less noticeable.

Similar advice can be given for coaches. For example, plastic coaches may be easier to paint before assembly. This especially cuts down the risk from masking if you are planning to fix it all together inseparably. If it is an etched kit, then make the underframe and roof so that they can be attached separately; I always do. Door and commode handles invariably get in the way of lining, so can they be attached later? It may be possible to tin the inside of the coach at the handle positions then fix the handles with 70° solder without affecting the finished paintwork. The various door and commode handles can easily be fixed to plastic models after painting.

By the way, if your model has lining on the door ventilators, as so many pre-grouping coaches had, then make sure the vents are stuck on absolutely in line. In fact they are best left off until after the coach side has been lined, as invariably there is insufficient room to line around the panel that the vent sits in.

Seriously think about painting a locomotive chassis before any lubricants are introduced. Plan the chassis construction to cater for this. Outside valve gear should always be made demountable, as should the outside cylinder/slidebar assembly. If you are spray painting the wheels, do so before assembly.

Self-quartering wheels, (eg. Romford/Markit, Slater's or AGH) can always be removed later and so give you more freedom as to when to paint, but non-quartering such as Ultrascale, Sharman or Gibson should not be taken off the axle once quartered. If you do intend painting the chassis at a later stage, then, at least, paint the chassis behind the wheels or use a keeper plate system so that wheels and axle boxes drop out as a unit.

Any enclosed voids should have drainage holes drilled. Sometimes the tender tank, and very often, the smokebox saddle, are fully enclosed boxes that will be penetrated by water during the washing process, but that water will take a long time to evaporate out.

Avoid weighting the engine until after painting. A heavy engine, especially in the larger scales, will be difficult to hold during spraying and may well want to roll around the bench during lining. Prepare the weights during construction but devise a way to fix them after painting. Weights fitted before washing will increase the number of water traps in the model, which slows down the drying process.

A number of detail parts are particularly vulnerable during the lining/detail painting stage when the model is lying on its side or even held between the knees (it happens). I find I frequently have to strengthen step plates below the footplate, especially when the middle step fits into a half-etched groove. Lamp brackets, whistles and other slender parts that project above the general level of the body need protection when the model is on its back. It is worth substituting a lamp bracket made from strip in place of one that has etched fold lines; the former is much stronger. The tall lamp brackets on ex LBSC locomotives are especially vulnerable during cleaning.

Buffers should be removable. The buffers should be off the model during initial general painting and especially when painting the buffer beams and housings, but they will give excellent protection to the rims of the housings, which are extremely vulnerable to knocks and abrasion, during the remainder of the painting and lining, so put them back in. Similarly, use demountable couplings so that they can be re-attached after painting.

If your locomotive kit has a resin superstructure, it is worthwhile doing two things before sticking any bits onto it. Firstly, give it a thorough clean with a toothbrush and abrasive cleaner to remove any remnants of mould release agents, which have a particular aversion to paint. Secondly, examine it closely with a magnifying glass to check for surface smoothness. I have found that some resins are not as smooth as they should be and give a poor finish compared to adjacent brass parts. It is far easier to rub down the resin surface before you add delicate brass parts to it.

Finally, test your locomotive before painting. Make sure it will go round corners. There is no excuse for cutting and carving after painting.

PROTOTYPE LIVERIES AND PHOTOGRAPHS

If you have built your model, you will, ideally, have used the kit instructions and diagrams together with photographs of the real thing. When it comes to painting, you will need photographs of a clean engine/coach/whatever, preferably dated, so that the lining and position of numbers and lettering, etc, is clearly visible.

You may not get the perfect set of photos, so you need to study the livery style of your railway for that date and get the general feel of the logic behind it as there are areas of the locomotive or coach that were never photographed, or are always in shade, so that the details cannot be picked out. You will also have to train yourself to not only look, but see; it is so easy to miss details because you're not concentrating. If you cannot find a particular livery detail, you may need to study photographs of other classes of vehicle in the same livery to find the clues that you need.

If you have a written specification for the livery you will still need to read between the lines and interpolate a bit, as these are rarely fully comprehensive. Some railways changed some aspect of their livery every couple of years (eg. the Great Western) while others were remarkably consistent over decades (eg, the London & North Western) (which probably explains why the latter is very well documented and the former poorly).

There are a number of published livery specifications and publications purporting to define the liveries of this railway or that, but, without exception, they all fall short of the full picture. The only way is to study photographs, once you know what the basic colours are and the dates of changes in style.

Beware of colour photographs! They may be suitable for establishing which bit is which colour but on *no account whatever* use them for matching colours. Different camera film or digital interpretation and printing methods can distort colour considerably, as can light and shade.

If you are copying a preserved engine and are reasonably sure that the livery is correct, then take some detailed photos, not just the usual three-quarter front view. Each part that is lined should have its own photograph, broadside on. Note where the changes of colour occur, including inside the cab, measure the lining, make a tracing of a lining corner. Measure edge distances and lining corner radii.

Many books contain photographs of locomotives in 'works grey'. These photographs served two purposes. One use was publicity and for this the locomotive may have been given considerable embellishment in terms of lining out. The other purpose was as a reference for the paint shop for the actual livery to be carried and these photographs may well have the correct livery. The problem is that the photo caption will not say how authentic the works grey livery is.

Many monochrome photographs do not differentiate between reds and black so red lining does not show up.

There are particular difficulties with coaches in that they weren't photographed as often as locomotives and the specialist books will illustrate them in their 'as-built' livery or 'as-scrapped' so that intermediate liveries are not shown.

Know your prototype. As long-lived machines, locomotives were modified periodically so that their external form may be very specific to a particular period – which may not suit your desired livery.

Do not work from undated material and do not trust interpretations by others. This includes copying the liveries of preserved vehicles. There is only one steam locomotive in this country that carries an authentic British Railways livery and that is 46235, *City of Birmingham*, which is in the 'Thinktank' (*sic*) in Birmingham This locomotive is in BR lined green livery, as

How not to do it – big time. Recently restored to working order after many months of painstaking work by the team, Lord Nelson is pictured here at Minehead station on the West Somerset Railway. The style of the lettering, the engine number, E850 and the cabside number plates are all correct for the period up to 1931, after which all Southern locomotives were renumbered. An engine of that period would have been painted in Maunsell's 'Dark Olive', not the Bulleid 'Malachite' seen here. I can appreciate the painting of a locomotive in an anachronistic livery, eg. Flying Scotsman, providing that the livery is correct in itself but, in my opinion, Lord Nelson is just a mix up. If the colour was the primary concern, then Bulleid-style markings should have been used. The lesson for model painters is to make sure that you know your period. Most of the information is out there, in fact we are lucky that so much is recorded.

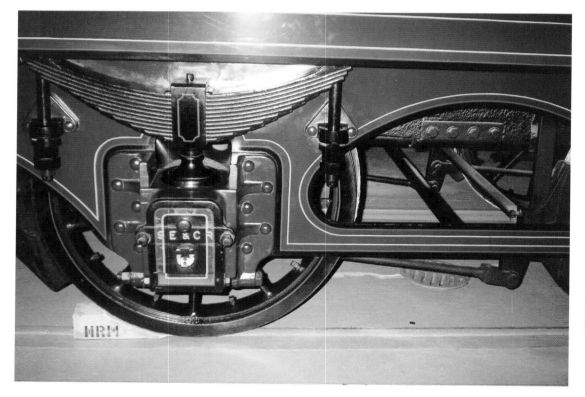

Wainwright Class D detail. This is one of the detail photographs I used to paint the model.

This 00 gauge model of LT&SR No. 80, Thundersley was scratchbuilt by Mike Edge. The livery is a little gaudy, I think. This is a case where the model that I have painted is the only time that I have seen the livery. I haven't seen the elusive preserved engine and so had little idea what to expect. The lettering of the name is only 1mm high and there is no easy way of doing it. I found the centre of the arc by trial and error and then drew two arcs of paint dots 1mm apart. I started in the middle of the word and added letters each side until I reached the T and Y.

Mike Edge built this 00 gauge ex North Eastern Dock Shunter from his own Judith Edge kit. It is not easy to find photographs of these engines as they were generally out of public view. The one in the NRM is painted in a different style but there were sufficient details in the relevant volume of RCTS Locomotives of the LNER to enable me to complete it.

withdrawn, apart from some touching up – in a different shade of green! It is our only absolute record of a BR steam era livery. Even the premier league of preserved railways and the National Railway Museum make mistakes.

The BR steam period itself is a minefield for livery variations. Consider this example for green engines. Valances (footplate angle, platform angle, hanging bar) were to be green, lined on the lower edge in black, $\frac{1}{2}$in wide with a $\frac{1}{8}$in orange line $\frac{1}{2}$in above that. That was the official edict. In practice, the position of the orange line varied depending on the depth of the valance, and the works doing the painting The BR

Standards and the rebuilt Bulleid Pacifics differed in that they had a continuous orange loop, and no black, on their deep valances.

On the Western Region, the valances were plain green. However, when Swindon painted its allocation of Standard Class 4 and 5 4-6-0s in lined green the valances were lined on the lower edge in black with orange, therefore conforming with neither the previous WR style nor the official style for BR Standard locomotives. When *Evening Star* was first turned out from Swindon, it had the bottom edge of its valances lined with a black line, above which was a single orange line. At a repaint

in 1967 at Crewe, it was given an orange loop. In 1981 during a repaint at the Great Western Museum, Didcot, it was given a single orange line just above the bottom edge, but no black edging, and this is how the locomotive is now exhibited at the NRM.

On the Eastern Region the valance lining continued vertically at the junction of valance and buffer beam (buffer plank) but from the late 1950s the black edge was omitted.

During the BR steam era there was a variety of interpretations of the standard schemes, even within each region, right through to the end in 1968. For example,

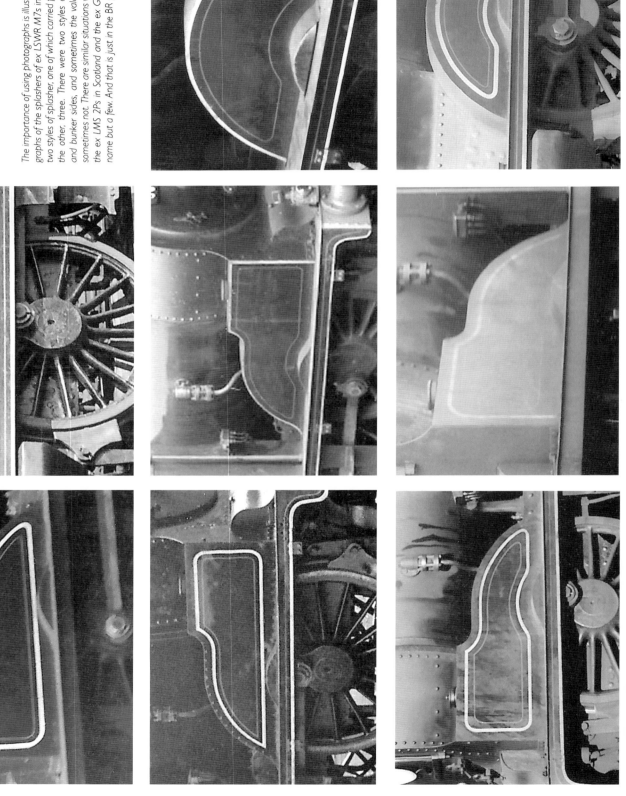

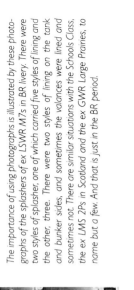

The importance of using photographs is illustrated by these photographs of ex LSWR M7s in BR livery. There were two styles of splasher, one of which carried five styles of lining and the other, three. There were two styles of lining on the tank and bunker sides, and sometimes the valances were lined and sometimes not. There are similar situations with the Schools Class, the ex LMS 2Ps in Scotland and the ex GWR Large Prairies, to name but a few. And that is just in the BR period.

there are at least six different ways of lining out the splasher/sandbox on an ex LSWR M7 in BR livery.

Finally, if you model the BR steam period, learn which way the lion faced and where it was applied! These are the rules: the first emblem (the Cycling Ferret) which, heraldically, was not a crest, was experimental from mid 1948, and used from 1949 – late 1956. On steam locomotives it always faced the front. On multiple units it was only used on motored vehicles. If the vehicle was also a driving vehicle, it faced the driving end; if it was not a driving vehicle it faced left. On single units it faced left. On the few double-ended diesel and electric locomotives it faced left,

mostly. It was not used on WR diesel railcars or locomotive-hauled stock.

The second emblem (the Ferret and Dartboard), which was a crest and was approved by the College of Arms, first appeared in summer 1956 and lasted until the last of the green engines was painted in Rail Blue. For the first six months of use, left-and right-facing versions were used in the same way as the first emblem. After that only the left-facing version was used, but engines that had received the right-facing version continued to carry it until the next repaint or scrapping.

The coaching stock roundel version of the crest was used on BR Standard corridor coaches, Mk Is and early Mk IIs, pre-BR

First Class coaches and special vehicles (restaurants and sleepers, etc), only on coaches in the crimson lake livery. On multiple units it was placed in the same position as the first emblem.

The above information is given with the following caveat – which applies to any so-called definitive statement you may read about liveries. 'Always' means 'mostly' and 'never' means 'except sometimes'. If you think the history of steam era liveries is complex, then pity the poor diesel modeller – there are over three hundred variations of the Class 47 livery – and still counting!

Do the research!

This beautiful 7mm scale M7 was one of a pair built by John Edwards which were the subject of an article in MRJ. These detail photographs show another variation of the splasher lining and how the BR lining generally is improved by the addition of the cream line.

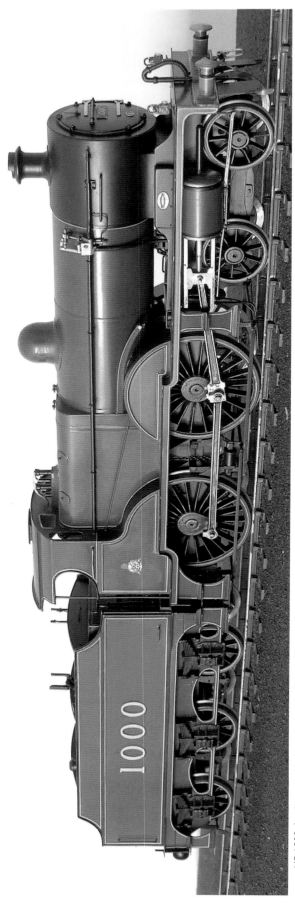

MR 1000. Another scratchbuilt model by Mike Edge in O gauge. Painted in PP Midland Crimson Lake, with reasonably straightforward lining, the most difficult part was getting all the 0's of the number in line. Care has to be taken in setting out any number containing the figure 1, where it is not the middle number. It takes up a ¼ space whereas all the other digits take a full space.

MR 1757. Another elegant 4-4-0 in O gauge, built by Mike Edge. This one is in the most flamboyant of the Midland liveries, known as the 'decorated' style with lots of crimson areas and lining. It took a long time but it was a pleasure to develop the livery from the plain as sprayed to the full glory – almost like bringing something to life. The brass numbers are by Slater's, attached with varnish after painting.

CHAPTER TWO
PREPARATION

This section covers preparing the material of the model so that it is ready to accept paint.

Steel is the material to which paint adheres best; non-ferrous metals come a long way behind. A lot depends on the condition of the metal surface, as oxidation, dirt and grease severely reduce the ability of the paint to stick. Brass, our most common modelling metal, has a particularly smooth surface to which paint has difficulty sticking.

There are a number of things that gang up on you during the construction phase to make painting difficult. The ones that affect paint adhesion and appearance are, in no particular order –

flux
solder blobs and fillets
glue snots (a technical term, used in the construction industry)
fibre-glass bristles
metal filings
grease
dust
tarnish

The assembly faults that affect the look of the finished model are mould lines, pitting of mouldings, misaligned parts, non right-angles, gaps and etching cusps and tabs.

Each time you do any construction work, the model should be cleaned at the end of the session – this will limit flux residues, which would otherwise become more and more inaccessible as the model becomes more complex. It is a good idea to build the model in separate modules, which can be cleaned easily, before finally fixing them irrevocably together.

Avoid using paste fluxes for soldering, as they are difficult to remove. I use dilute phosphoric acid instead but, unless it is washed off, it will simply turn itself into concentrated phosphoric acid and eat away into the brass, producing a nice green deposit.

The tools and materials I use for cleaning up are

a chisel
a small sharpened screwdriver
dental scrapers
the usual Swiss files
fine emery paper
scalpel
half-inch paint brush

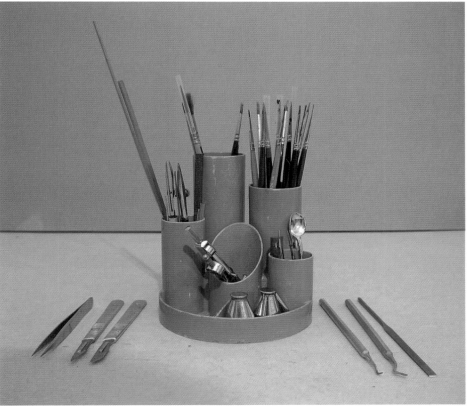

The useful desk tidy holds my brushes, pens, dividers (stored points down), compasses, paint cups (also stored upside-down to keep dust out) and other bits and pieces. To the right are two sizes of dental scrapers and the Swiss file converted to a chisel, and on the left are curved and straight blade scalpels and fine tweezers.

fibre-glass brushes
limescale remover
'Flash' liquid or similar equivalent
cellulose thinners

I also use 'cream' cleaners, such as 'Shiny Sinks' if the model is particularly yucky, but it can leave a powdery deposit that needs a thorough washing off with running water and a soft brush. I do not use washing-up liquids as they contain lanolin, which is kind to the hands but not to paint adhesion. However, having said that, other well-known modellers swear by the stuff.

The chisel is fashioned from an old flat Swiss file with a sharp edge ground on the end. It is the tool I use most out of all my tools. It will remove solder fillets from internal corners, it will pare down or scrape off solder and glue snots, it will take lumps off the surface of paint without disturbing the paint – incredibly useful. The sharpened screwdriver does the same job but in places the chisel is too wide to reach. Provided there are no rivets, the emery (1200 grade) will smooth out solder deposits to a negligible thickness – it does not need to disappear completely.

Paint will stick best to a surface that is rough at a microscopic level. This can be achieved by etching, abrasive cleaners, grit blasting or abrading with emery or fibre-glass brush.

It follows that areas of the model surface that are half-etched are sufficiently 'micro-rough' and need no further action except for making sure they are clean and degreased. It is possible to clean and etch a flat-sided model, such as a flush-sided coach, with ferric chloride, which is the chemical used by the etching industry. This will clean the parts and give an excellent key for the paint, but don't let them stay in contact with the etchant for too long or you will have no metal left to paint. I have used this very effective method for 4mm coaches but I lack a container large enough for bigger vehicles.

Grit blasting is a very good method of both surface cleaning and providing a key in one operation. Badger do a 'Hobby Abrasive Gun', which is quite effective on small areas, and other types for the occasional user are available from such as 'Machine Mart'. Abrasive guns really need to be used in an enclosed cabinet so that the aluminium oxide powder can be collected for re-use and not be spread far and wide. I have an abrasive gun (but no cabinet) that I use on discrete parts of the model that are difficult to clean by other means but, because of the dust created, I have to use it outside the house.

The model must be absolutely bone dry before grit blasting so that the powder

doesn't stick. The residues must be cleared out with both brush and high-pressure air from the air brush. Plastic models can also be grit blasted to provide a key for the paint, but be gentle.

If you propose to use an abrasive gun on a regular basis, it is worthwhile seeking out a commercial supplier of fine-grade aluminium oxide, as buying small quantities from hobby suppliers can be expensive. Similarly, a commercial gun would be a better prospect than a 'hobby' gun.

Smooth surfaces on the model can be abraded with fine 'wet and dry', used dry, but should there be any surface features, such as rivets, that prevent this, then the best tool is the fibre-glass brush. I use the

4mm pen type, which allows me to make an impression without undue pressure and will reach most areas. The big disadvantage of using the fibre-glass brush is the residue of fibres, which take on a life of their own on release from the confines of the pen. They get in your fingers unless you've had the foresight to wear protective gloves, but worse than that, they will reappear at all stages of the painting process.

Once you are satisfied that all surface blemishes have been dealt with, the model now has to be made squeaky clean. I use a three stage process for brass models and two stage for other metals.

Stage one for all models is a wash in an alkaline solution. I use Flash All Purpose

These photos of a 7mm scale brass coach side show the before and after effects of blasting with aluminium oxide powder. Certainly cleaner, with the desired micro-roughness required for good paint adhesion. But every silver lining has a cloud – it's an amazingly messy business without a cabinet to contain the particles (and also to collect them for re-use). I reserve this process for the badly tarnished model that has taken someone ten years to build, or has been sitting around for a similar period waiting to be painted. I put on overalls, hat, gloves and goggles and do it in the garden. Without that protection it's a shower and change of clothes afterwards.

detergent or similar equivalent, which, as a wetting agent, should lift any solid matter that is not actually stuck to the metal and also, being alkaline (Flash has a pH of 9.5), neutralise any remaining flux. I place the model in a washing up bowl and spray the detergent neat from a spray bottle. I then work it into all the corners with a half inch paint brush. You could use a tooth brush but I find the bristles are too short and can knock off small details. Also, with the bristles being at right-angles to the handle, it won't get into corners. Follow this stage with a good rinse, as the detergent is only a wetting agent, it's the water that does the washing. The washing-up bowl is essential to catch any part that may be knocked off the model.

Stage two. If the model is brass, the second stage is limescale remover or, if the brass is well tarnished, 'Shiny Sinks' or similar abrasive cleaner. These are slightly acidic, so wear rubber gloves. They clean the tarnish off the brass but unfortunately blacken whitemetal and solder. This is not a detriment – it just looks unattractive. This stage is not necessary for whitemetal or nickel-silver models, or after grit blasting. Do not use limescale remover on steel or aluminium as it rusts the former and attacks the latter.

If you do intend to attack the model with some vigour during the acid wash stage, I would strongly recommend hand and face protection as the droplets of the cleaner can make you itch for hours!

Stage three. The final stage is a wash in cellulose thinners to remove any last remaining grease and finger prints, especially for the chassis if it has been lubricated. This should be done in a well-ventilated area where the smell will not enter the house. If it's a plastic model use white spirit or paraffin. If you don't fancy the idea of washing in thinners, then, as an alternative, brush it on liberally with a half-inch brush, wipe off what you can, then leave in a well-ventilated space to evaporate off. Repeat.

Although household cleaners are marketed as being 'grease removers' or 'tough on grease' they are only designed to move animal fats and then only mild deposits. They do this by reducing the surface tension of water so that it can flow under the deposit and float it off. Degreasing agents like cellulose thinners actually dissolve the oil or grease so that it is washed off or evaporates.

After the first two stages, use lots, and I mean lots, of water to rinse while rubbing vigorously with a half-inch paint brush.

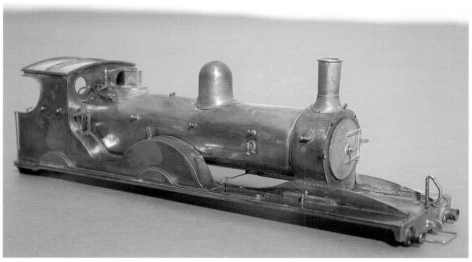

This is the state in which I received this 4mm scale T3. Fairly clean but the brass shows evidence of discoloration and tarnishing.

The engine was photographed after cleaning with 'Shiny Sinks'. The brasswork has been left tarnish free and is ready for painting.

Stage one should be left to dry thoroughly so that any chemical reaction with stray flux becomes apparent. This will be in the form of a light greeny-blue deposit, which will need to be scraped off and brushed away.

Make sure the model is thoroughly dry before proceeding to the next stage, which is priming. Enclosed voids and laminations are particularly troublesome to dry out as water will find its way in but will be reluctant to evaporate. If in doubt leave it for 24 hours in a warm dry place.

It is possible to accelerate the drying process by heating the model with a hair dryer but, as mentioned above, beware of laminations and voids, which may contain trapped water. It is a good idea to turn up the pressure in the air-brush and fire air at areas that may hold water. Such areas are the joint between dome or chimney and boiler, around the smokebox saddle, around the cab fittings, in fact any part fitted to the basic body. The action of the air will chase out any water – you'll be surprised how much is in there.

If you have used an abrasive cleaner, take care when blowing water off, as it will leave streaks of the cleaner on the surface. This needs to be wiped off immediately with a cloth or paper towel.

After rinsing and drying, you will probably find that the areas of solder have developed a light grey deposit on the surface. This is the result of a chemical reaction between the solder and cleaning fluids. This will have to be scraped off and brushed away; if you wash the model again it will recur.

You could leave the fibre-glass brushing stage until after the washing so that you can deal with surface deposits and tarnish in the one hit. BUT the model must be absolutely dry. Clean off the glass fibres with high-pressure air from the airbrush.

Now that the model is clean do not touch it with your hands; wear latex or polythene gloves to put it under a ventilated dust cover to continue drying before moving on to the priming.

STRIPPING

If you are repainting a model and are not happy with the condition of the paint on it, or wish to use cellulose paint (or spray can car acrylics) on a model previously painted in enamels, then you are faced with stripping off the existing paint. It is neither pleasant nor easy to do this. If you are determined to go ahead, wear suitable gloves, as paint strippers are caustic and will sting the skin on the back of your hands. Another reason to wear gloves is that the stripped paint will stick to your hands in a random unattractive fashion.

There are a number of methods to use, all of which create a mess. First of all try scraping. If the model is made from brass and has been badly painted, it may be that the painter did not clean it up beforehand, so the paint may readily come off with a suitable flat scraper. Even if it doesn't all come off, you will have reduced the amount to be attacked with a chemical stripper.

Provided the model is not plastic, cellulose thinners are a good way of removing any of the three types of paint we use. The drawbacks are the smell and the disposal of the spent solution. You need a container large enough to hold the item to be stripped, somewhere where the smell does not matter, a wide-necked container for the thinners and a half inch paint brush. You may wish to wear a face mask as well.

Liberally brush the thinners over the model and you will see the paint pucker up and crack. If the model has more than one layer of paint you will have to keep wetting it until the metal shows through. The worst part is getting paint out of the corners and openings, but it must all be removed. Once stripped, leave the model somewhere to dry off before bringing it back in to your living quarters. The remnants of the thinners and paint mess should be emptied into a container and placed somewhere so that the thinners can evaporate away. They are going to evaporate anyway, but better in your garden shed than in the drains.

The other method for metal models is to use a paint stripper such as Nitromors or a DIY store own brand. These are generally in a gel form but Nitromors 'Craftsman' is a liquid. Pour a bit out of the can into the lid and jab it on with the brush. The problem is getting rid of the yucky paint/gel mix. The mix is sticky and cannot be readily washed off with water and if water comes into contact with the gel there is a reaction that gives off a gas that will sting your eyes. What I do is spray on neat detergent, which releases the goo, and then wash it off with water, keeping my head out of the way. Alternatively white spirit or meths can be used. After using this method, examine your model thoroughly when it is dry, as the stripper can dry out in less accessible parts of the model and produce an interesting effect on your subsequent paint work.

For plastic and metal models, a gentle stripper, such as Superstrip from Phoenix Precision, can be used. This is non-caustic, water soluble and biodegradable. These types are slow to work and the model will need to be kept wrapped in cling film for a day or so. They are, however, much more pleasant to work with.

Some plastic RTR stock is not affected by paint strippers. In this case a gentle rub-down of any rough areas is all that is required before painting.

Whichever chemical is used, it will attack glues such as Araldite and Evo-stik so any part thus attached will either come away or the bond be weakened. Make sure you examine the model after stripping and retrieve any bits that have fallen off.

I hate stripping – and charge a lot for it. After all I could be doing something more pleasant, like lining the front end of a streamlined Crimson Princess Coronation.

PRECAUTIONS AND THE SPRAYING AREA

I am lucky enough to have my own workshop with windows on two elevations. I have removed the opening window from one frame and replaced it with a sheet of ply containing a 6in diameter, 150 watt extractor fan. This fan efficiently removes all the fumes from the work area and, if the windows and door are closed, produces a partial vacuum in the room.

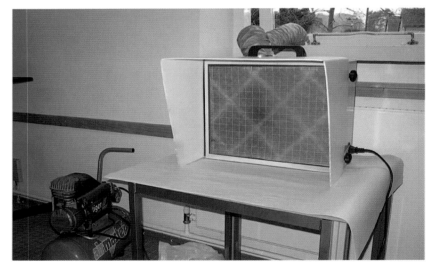

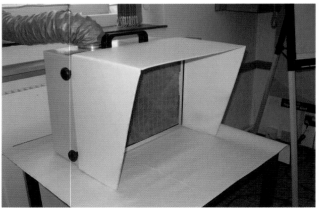

This is the GraphicAir Systems filter and extractor cabinet, model A300S–D, from Widespread Solutions Ltd. It has a hose attachment, which can be seen trailing out through the window. Recirculating types are also available.

The alternative mechanical system is the spray booth, which is rather like a cooker hood on its side. These are available commercially or you could make your own using a fan of sufficient power – bathroom fans are not powerful enough.

Adequate ventilation is of extreme importance as fumes from paint and thinners can be toxic. If there is no extract system or spray booth, then painting outside the house is the only option. It is quite feasible to paint in the open air but it severely limits painting to fine, warm and still days. The other option is to use the garage or shed provided a through draught is available. Obviously, spray with the wind, not against it. Temperature control is a problem outside the controlled environment of the house but at least start with a thermometer so you know how big a problem it is. The spraying area must be warm.

If you can smell the paint you are breathing it. Some protection from the fumes is vital if there is no forced ventilation. A face mask, which has organic fume filters (usually charcoal), is necessary as simple dust masks are no use at all. There are numerous masks on the market, which cost between £24 – £30; my own came from Halfords, ready fitted with fume filters. A disposable folding type, similar to a dust mask, but containing a charcoal filter and suitable for up to six hours, can be found at some DIY stores. It pays to read the small print on the instructions as sometimes this is at variance with what is says on the packaging.

Paint thinners and fumes therefrom are highly flammable and can be ignited by electrical sparks. Modern extractor fans have brushless induction motors and are therefore safe from sparking. If you intend to use a hairdryer to accelerate the drying of paint, only use it at low settings, where the heating element does not glow red.

My spraying stand is not at all sophisticated. For years it was a large cardboard box on top of a small table. Now it is a wooden box on the same table. Oh yes, and there's a piece of newspaper on top of that. On top of the newspaper I lay a piece of chipboard on which the model sits. I have a number of bits of chipboard and mdf in three basic sizes; the largest will just take a 7mm 'Princess', the middle one a 4mm engine or 7mm tender, and the smallest, a 4mm tender. They don't have to be chipboard, of course, any thin bit of wood or mdf will do provided it is strong enough to

The personal safety equipment. The mask I wear when spraying is the twin filter type, this particular one being bought at Halfords for about £25. There are a number of models on the market at a range of prices. The soft mask is a Wickes one, with a charcoal filter which has a life of about 8 hours. The latex gloves can be found in supermarkets (but not our local Sainsbury's), hardware stores or automotive accessory shops. They are generally a single-use item.

Painting stand. This is as crude as they come, a piece of 3mm MDF that came as a piece of packing in a flat pack. It was cut to accommodate a 4mm Pacific in length and has two small blocks glued on to form a cradle for the curved cab roof. The engine on the stand is an LNWR Chopper tank that has had its etching primer applied. The solder patches on the underside are still visible through the primer. This is not a problem.

take the weight of your heaviest model. I find that this system is very manoeuvrable and a model can be taken right to the edge of the box, allowing me to get in close from most angles. Also, when spraying is finished, to avoid touching it, the item stays on its bit of wood as it is transferred to the drying area.

I generally use the stand for priming and 'all over' finishes. For laying on top coats, I hold the model while wearing a latex glove. This gives me the freedom to turn the model as I wish, to do the sides, top, inside the cab and underside of boiler all in one session. I would not recommend a circular turntable to place the model on for painting, as this will limit your freedom to get in close with the paint spray. There are purpose-made holding tools available but, as an engineer, I would suggest that these are of little use except for the lightest of plastic models.

LIGHTING AND VISION AIDS

You will need to consider the lighting requirements for two situations – spraying, and detail work at the bench/table/desk. The requirements for each situation are quite different.

When spraying, it is essential not only to see what you are doing, but also to have light reflected off the surface of the paint, so that you can see exactly what is happening as the paint lands. Part of the spraying process is to watch the droplets of paint coalesce to form a completely blemish-free surface, and this process is made more visible by the reflection of light from the wet surface. I have an Anglepoise lamp positioned to my right and higher than my spraying hand, set up to reflect light off the model.

For general painting at the bench, positioning lights is a far more difficult proposition. Wherever the general room lighting is positioned, your head, or the hand that holds the brush or pen, will always seem to put the point of contact into the shade. Ideally one needs a soft light at the eleven o'clock position (for right-handed people), sufficiently low for it not to be blocked by the painter's head. If the light is too strong, it will create deep shadows and harsh reflections, so quite a puny light is required.

Natural daylight is good provided it is not too strong – facing out in a north-facing bay window would perhaps be best in the domestic situation. Something to be borne in mind when you next decide to move house!

One of the problems facing the modeller from the age of 40 on is increasing long-sightedness, loss of ability to change focus and reduced vision at lower light levels. Looking around the various exhibition halls that I visit, I see that the majority of visitors are, like me, grey haired, so, to put it kindly, ours is a mature gentlemen's hobby.

There are a number of vision aids on the market for various amounts of the hard-earned. For those of you just joining the ranks of the long-sighted, a pair of ready-made reading glasses from the High St. chemist or supermarket will magnify the work sufficiently for you. Choose the cheapest and most comfortable; they are not a fashion item.

As long-sightedness really sets in, a visit to the optician will be necessary. For the model maker I think that mono-focal lenses are a must as bi- or multi-focal glasses require you to hold your head in a particular position, which can be a literal pain in the neck. Tell the optician that you need strong reading glasses for close work, or, if you're feeling reckless and enjoy living life on the edge, tell him you are into model trains.

For higher magnifications there are magnifying glasses on stands, some with built-in lights, clip-on magnifiers for spectacles, and visors. The Squires catalogue lists numerous varieties from £15 to £100. I use a visor called Head Loupe, which came with four strengths of lens, and is quite comfortable to wear. It took a bit of getting used to but now I would be lost without it. I think a bench-mounted magnifying glass is rather limiting and an illuminated one would generate heat, which will reduce the workability time of lining paints. The choice is yours.

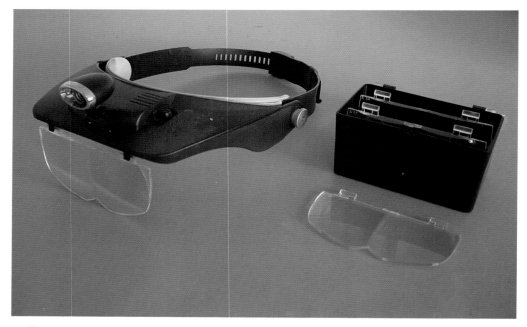

This is my head loupe, now rather battered after some seven years of use. It comes with four different lenses, of which I now use the third strongest. I have never used the light on the top as I found the visor a bit heavy with the batteries in. However, if you can cope with that, you can choose either a filament bulb version or a more expensive multi-LED version. The Squires catalogue lists five types of visor and numerous magnifying spectacles and glasses.

CHAPTER THREE
PRIMING

Before doing this, the preparation continues! Check that the model is dry. Give it a close inspection, as this may be the last chance to correct any assembly errors. Look particularly for deposits on soldered areas and lurking glass fibres – especially inside cabs, around footsteps and other angles.

If the model has been thoroughly cleaned, as outlined above, paint will stick to it without a primer. In fact the vast majority of models running today have not been primed and, apart from exposed edges, the paint is still in place.

Before we go any further, I think we need to define what a 'primer' is. Primers have three jobs to do in the real world, not necessarily all at the same time. The principal use of a metal primer is the prevention of rust on steel. This is what your average aerosol car primer does, as it contains a rust inhibitor, which is usually zinc phosphate. The primer does NOT have improved paint adhesion. It is designed for use on steel, to which paint adheres well anyway. When used on non-ferrous metals it is no more than an undercoat.

Having said that, a good even coat of aerosol primer gives a nice even base to

work from as it hides all colour variations below it. The most common method of undercoating/priming is to use a commercial aerosol car spray, either grey, red oxide or white. For red or black engines, use oxide, other colours grey, and for white coach roofs use white.

The second type is the 'filler primer', which contains a high proportion of solids and is designed to fill minor depressions, scratches and the like. They are meant to be rubbed down after application, so if you cannot do this because of other surface features, like rivets, they should be avoided.

The 'real' primer is etching primer, which has an important job to do on non-ferrous metals. After application, an acid in the mix, over a period of 12 – 24 hours, eats into the metal surface, creating the microscopic roughness that the paint requires to improve its adhesion.

AEROSOL PRIMERS

It is essential that you have practised using aerosol paint and learned what it can and can't do. Different makes of paint have different spray patterns, either a cone or fan. I have generally used Halfords cans,

principally because the nearest supplier to me is Halfords, but I'm sure other types are as good. It doesn't matter which you use so long as you learn how to use them and know their limitations. By the way, if there are instructions on the back of the can, read them.

For best results, the model, paint and room should be warm. A warm model will have a dryer surface than a cold one. When the paint is released from the pressure of the can it loses a considerable amount of energy and it does this by rapidly cooling. Once the paint is on the model it needs to start to dry, which it will do quicker if things are warm. If spraying with an aerosol, I generally have the hair dryer playing warm (not hot) air onto the model. This keeps things warm and also blows the spray away from me.

First, shake the can for two minutes from when the stirring ball starts to rattle. Test the spray on a piece of paper/card/metal to see if it is behaving itself. If it is, it is time to warm it up. I put some hot tap water into a measuring jug and then put the aerosol can in it. If the can is part used, it may well float, so I weight it down with an

All the parts for the Patriot laid out after cleaning, ready for the etching primer to go on.

Spraying on the etching primer with an air brush – this was before I acquired the spray gun. My extract fan mesh looks like it needs another clean.

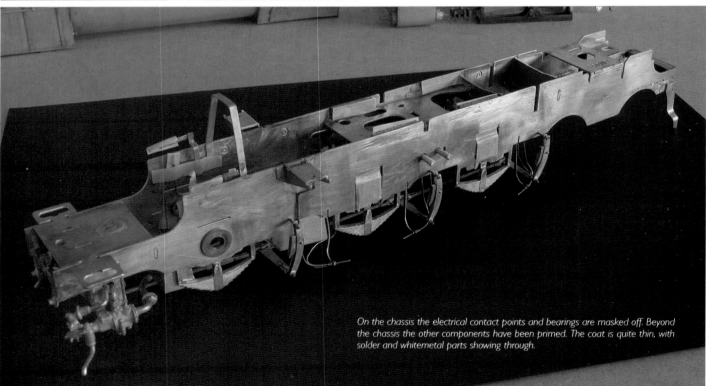

On the chassis the electrical contact points and bearings are masked off. Beyond the chassis the other components have been primed. The coat is quite thin, with solder and whitemetal parts showing through.

upturned mug. The water must be no hotter than you would use to have a wash – I don't want to be responsible for exploding paint cans, but the paint is best if it is really quite warm. While the paint is warming, the model needs to be removed from under cover and placed in position for spraying. Because aerosol cans have such a wide spray and are delivering a lot of paint, I would put the model on a stand, propped up with, and on, blocks. Also, when doing the underside, there is nowhere to hold the model, so putting it on to something that is easily moved around, as mentioned previously, is the best option.

When the model is ready and checked for dust, fibreglass bristles, etc, retrieve the paint can, dry it off if it has been in water, then give it another shake for half a minute or so. Test and GO.

Spray the underside first. This is not just to test your patience but has good practical reasons. Most importantly, when you turn the model over to paint the top, the only scuffing will be to the underside of footsteps, etc, which is far less critical than, say, the cab roof if you did it the other way around. Secondly, it needs doing anyway. Thirdly, it's an area that can get forgotten. Fourthly, it puts a coat of primer on the underside of foot steps, handrails, etc. Finally, it allows practice on the job before the more important top side is done.

Spray from about six to nine inches (150 – 225 mm) and move STEADILY from one end to the other. If you spray from too great a distance, the paint will be dry before it hits the model and you will get a 'sand paper' finish, OK for station platform surfaces but not rolling stock. The actual rate at which you move will depend on what you have learnt about the paint during practice sessions. Start and stop the spray OFF the model. Do NOT dwell or you will get runs and 'curtains'. If there are areas of shadow which are difficult to get paint into, build up the paint a bit at a time, letting it dry for a couple of minutes between coats.

Try to spray in a regular pattern, stopping the spray after each stroke. This gives you time to see where the paint is landing, saves paint and avoids your waving the can around like a mad thing and getting paint everywhere. Cover all you can see on the side nearest to you and also inside the far side, then turn the model through 90° horizontally and spray the end near you and inside the far end; turn again, repeat for the other side and then the other end. Leave it to become touch dry, no less than ten minutes but an hour is better, then turn it over and spray the top side in the sane manner.

Spraying the top of a locomotive will be a more complex operation than the underside. The cab front, all around the dome and chimney, inside the cab and tender need to be done, before completing the remaining areas not already covered. The general rule when spraying is 'detail before general'.

Plastic models do not need priming for the top coats to stick, but if you have done any work on the body, a coat of matt undercoat/primer will help to show up any blemishes and gaps. Modern car primers can be used on plastics. If you intend to use a car paint aerosol for the finish colour on a plastic model I would recommend a full coat of primer as protection, just in case.

ETCHING PRIMER

An essential for non-ferrous metals and also resins is an etching primer. This is obtainable as an aerosol can or as a two-part etching primer from automotive paint suppliers or a similar product is obtainable from Phoenix Precision, either from shows or by mail order. The PP two-part primer consists of a 125ml bottle of activated thinners containing the etchant (phosphoric acid) and a 125ml can of paint. It says on the can that it is enamel paint but it behaves more like cellulose in that it dries very quickly and can only be shifted with cellulose thinners.

It is an extremely effective primer, which sticks like the proverbial, but I found that to spray it you have to ignore the instructions. It says that it should be thinned 1:1, but I tried that and all I got out of my airbrush were cobwebs. It must be thinned far more – I used two parts etching thinners plus one part of cellulose thinners to one part primer.

I used to use a single action airbrush for this, the Badger 200, set to give a fairly heavy flow and sprayed on in a similar manner to an aerosol. As I said, it dries almost as quickly as cellulose, so the model can be turned over for spraying to continue in a few minutes. Only a thin coat is necessary – it does not need to obliterate the various surface colours. Once it is dry it must be left for 24 hours for the etching process to work.

The etching primer is also an excellent primer for covering cast resin. Resins tend to reject paint that is too wet and thin. Spraying primer from an aerosol can onto resin may result in the primer gathering itself up into pools, and leaving bald patches in between. Spraying a primer from a spray gun or airbrush will allow you to put on a tack coat – this is explained more fully under 'Spraying with Enamels' – but basically it is a thin coat that is semi-dry on landing. Two or three tack coats will give the full primer coat something to grip, preventing bald patches.

I used the Badger 200 for two reasons. One I didn't want the acid to be etching the inside of my best airbrush, and two, it gave me a constant regulated flow.

Nowadays I use a two-part cellulose etching primer applied through a spray gun with a mix of two parts etching thinners to one part primer. This type can be recoated after twelve hours but I tend to leave it for twenty-four hours. These automotive primers can be found in your local car paint suppliers, not the chain stores like Halfords, but the company that supplies the car body repair shops.

When the primer is dry, check it over – closely, really closely. Now is the time that further glass fibres reveal themselves and should be removed. If there is any discoloration of the primer, possibly a glossy darkening along the inside of an angle, this would suggest that there is a damp area and the primer is not sticking. Rub it off, dry, rub down and respray. If the primer dries lighter in colour in some areas this would suggest residues under the primer from either neutralised flux or abrasives from cream cleaners. Again rub off, rub down and respray.

Check the general surface smoothness. The best tool for this is the lightest of touches with a dry finger. I find that a brisk rub with a dry half inch brush will take off any slight surface grittiness from aerosol undercoat/primers. Hopefully, earlier checks will have removed any gross surface blemishes but if they suddenly become apparent at this stage then you must deal with them now, it is easier than later. If this means rubbing down back to base metal then so be it.

Remember, the finish on your top coat will never be better than the finish on the primer.

The most common gloss paints. The popular Humbrol range of paints comes in 14 ml tinlets. Some colours are available in 120 ml cans, like the No. 85 Satin Black shown upper right. The paints used to be in every High Street but now, with model shops closing down, they are less easy to find. The whole range plus some of the larger cans are listed in the Squires catalogue. They are not railway specific, in fact they are aimed at the plastic aircraft, military hardware and ship modellers but some of their range is very useful for lining rolling stock. The only full range of railway colours in gloss enamel comes from Phoenix Precision. All the range is available by mail order and a limited range of Big Four + BR is generally available at the major shows. Apart from a few lining colours, the gloss enamels are only available in 50 ml and larger cans. The full range of dull and matt colours are usually available in 14 ml tinlets at shows. PP are introducing a range of acrylic paints to run alongside the enamel range. This is the smallest size of pot, which is 30 ml. Not illustrated are the range of paints marketed by Comet Models and Chris Wesson. Both these ranges are cellulose. Railmatch paints, now acrylic, are only available in satin and matt. The top view shows useful paint and jar holders which are available from P.P.

CHAPTER FOUR
PAINTING

All paints consist of pigment, binders and thinners. There may also be other additives that affect drying time, density, surface finish and workability. It is the binder that defines the type of paint – enamel, cellulose or acrylic.

ENAMEL

Enamel paints are also known as alkyd paints and have a binder made from synthetic or vegetable oils (eg linseed oil) plus the pigment and the thinners (turpentine or mineral [white] spirit). On drying, the alkyd oil oxidises and polymerises, that is the molecules join together and form long chains. Although touch dry in a few hours, the chemical reactions continue for some time. Depending on the thickness of the coat, it can take up to two weeks before most of the activity is complete and from that point on, because of the oxidation, the paint will not be dissolved by its original thinners. In practice, the surface of the paint is impervious to white spirit after a couple of days.

A second coat of paint applied after the first has fully cured will not have such a strong bond as paint applied 'wet on wet', although for models this is largely academic.

The perceived disadvantage of enamel paints is that they do take time to dry, but, in fact, this is a positive advantage. The advantages are

(1) that they can be brush painted, which makes touching up easy,
(2) any paint that goes where it is not wanted can be removed readily with white spirit, even 24 hours later, without affecting the cured paint below
(3) there is a full range of named railway colours in gloss, available from Phoenix-Precision
(4) they can used for lining through a suitable pen.

It is a common fallacy that to use enamels for lining, the base paint must be cellulose, or that to line on enamel, a water-based paint or ink must be used. It is simply not true.

CELLULOSE (LACQUER)

In cellulose paints, the binder is a cellulose compound (cellulose is extracted from wood). The thinner is mainly toluene. The paint dries through evaporation of the thinner so there is no change in the chemical nature of the paint on drying, so it will remain soluble in cellulose thinners. This means that a second coat of paint, applied after the first has cured, will bed itself into the original paint through surface softening. This produces a strong bond between the two layers.

The main advantage of cellulose paints is their rapid drying to a very smooth surface. The disadvantages are that there is only a limited range of railway colours available off the shelf and that brushing is difficult.

In terms of spraying, cellulose is the more tricky as it dries so quickly. If, for example, you are spraying a valance and haven't masked off the remainder, then paint that flies past the valance could have dried by the time it reaches the boiler side, where it will produce the 'sand paper' finish. Similar problems arise when working around a cab. With cellulose, spray distance and wetness of landing paint are critical. One technique is to use 'thug' painting – spray high volumes of the mix from a short distance but move quickly, and no finesse in corners, in fact just like using an aerosol.

Once the technique of spraying cellulose paint has been mastered, it is easier to obtain a smooth finish than with enamels or acrylics. The major disadvantage is that paint that goes where it shouldn't cannot be removed easily. If it is a light infestation and you are quick enough, it can be rubbed off with a cotton bud damp with white spirit. If it has dried, an abrasive cleaner such as T-Cut will remove it, but do it carefully so as not to damage the underlying paint. If it is a dense application, all that you can do is respray the area in the original colour.

ACRYLIC

Acrylic paints consist of pigment in an acrylic polymer emulsion, which can be thinned with water.

An emulsion is a mix of two, or more, liquids that do not dissolve each other. An example is oil in water. To make an emulsion of oil and water (for paint or for machine tool lubrication), the oil and water have to be mechanically battered into submission. The result is a mix of tiny drops of each liquid that appears to act like a solution.

Acrylic paints behave like domestic emulsion paints in that they dry quickly and, once dry, can only be dissolved with cellulose thinners or paint stripper. Their main advantage is that they are virtually odour-free and water soluble and therefore much safer for spraying. They can therefore be sprayed in locations where other paints would cause nuisance, for example in an apartment. Soft or distilled water can be used for spray thinners but a proprietary thinner is better as it contains agents (glycol or glycerine) that aid the smooth flow of paint once it has landed, giving a better finish. Paint that lands where it is not wanted can be removed with water, but only for a short time; once it has set, water or acrylic thinners won't touch it.

Acrylic paints can be used for lining but they will dry in the bow pen more quickly than enamels. Also, because of the quick drying, it is not possible to allow the paint to thicken up to give fine dense lines, as with enamels. You also lose the overwhelming advantage of enamel paints, that of being able to correct errors for up to 24 hours. It is not recommended to use acrylic paint in a tube pen.

COMPATIBILITY

Cellulose thinners will attack enamel and acrylic paints. Cellulose thinners, when sprayed onto cellulose paint, will soften the paint but, providing that there is no actual mechanical abrasion, will evaporate off and leave the paint unharmed – it will even improve the surface.

Cellulose paint cannot be put on top of either enamel or acrylic paint. Acrylic can be put on top of enamel and vice versa, and both can be put on cellulose.

PAINT PROBLEMS
Orange peel

Orange peel, the bane of painters, is a result of a combination of too high a surface tension and too quick a drying time. The paint lands in a random pattern of minute droplets; as paint continues to land on the surface, some lands in the spaces but some lands on, or touching, the paint that is already there. Larger drops are formed from the droplets that are in contact with each other and start a chain of 'hills and valleys' in the paint. If the paint is too viscous, it will not flow out to a level surface and the result is 'orange peel'.

There are a number of ways to defeat this. One is to increase the volume of paint so that more paint is going on more quickly,

Orange peel. This 4mm Patriot, not painted by me, has a severe attack of 'orange peel' caused by the paint being too viscous when it landed.

preventing the peaks from forming. Second is to add more thinners to reduce the viscosity and surface tension. Thirdly, a drop of matting agent will help reduce surface tension. Fourthly, make sure the paint is warm, as warm paint flows better.

If using enamel paints, orange peel can be defeated by laying on a 'dust' coat (also known as a tack coat or mist coat). The dust coat is a very thin coat sprayed at a very high air to paint ratio, and higher pressure, thus atomising the paint to very tiny droplets, giving a very even surface. This coat will in fact be semi-dry, but very fine. Once the area is covered, move straight in to the 'wet' coat. This is a higher paint to air ratio, high paint volume flooding the areas to be painted. It is also a very scary, high-risk strategy on the knife edge between success and disaster. At least it is if you do not practise. The presence of the dust coat gives the paint something to grip and so is marginally less likely to run, so you need to practise to find the minimum volume of paint required to give you the finish that you require.

Orange peel is less of a problem with cellulose paints as these are sprayed in much more dilute form.

Gritty paint

Gritty paint is another spraying problem. There are at least three causes. The first is by spraying from too great a distance so that the thinners have evaporated before the paint lands, so that it cannot flow. The second is a result of paint landing, drying and then being blown off and landing elsewhere on the model. The third, and most

difficult to eliminate, is when something gets in the way of the paint on its way to the surface. Such an obstruction could be a tall safety valve in front of the cab or something as thin as a hand rail. It will manifest itself as a gritty area on the front of the cab or behind boiler side hand rails.

The direction of spraying is important where there are obstructions. Spray from 45° above and below the hand rail position to get behind it. Where two surfaces meet at right-angles, e.g. cab and firebox, the least accessible of the two will tend to get a gritty surface. I don't quite know the reason for it but it's possibly due to the paint landing on it at a very acute angle. To prevent it happening, thug spray at an angle of 45° to both surfaces. Alternatively, each surface can be masked in turn and sprayed normally.

Gritty paint is mostly associated with cellulose spraying but I have seen very gritty enamel paint. The way to alleviate the problem, if it has already occurred, is to flood the surface of the paint with neat thinners sprayed at a low pressure (try 10 psi). This works on dried cellulose but the enamel must be recently sprayed and still wet for the technique to work. This softens the top surface of the paint and allows it to settle to a flat surface.

Unfortunately, this method does not work with acrylic paints. With acrylic and cured enamel, the only solution is to rub down with fine wet-and-dry, then put on a second coat more carefully than the first.

The gritty paint problem is best tackled by building your model as small units which can be fixed together after painting.

Striping

Striping occurs when the spray is close to the model so that only a thin strip is receiving paint. If the next run of paint does not overlap the paint that is already on, stripes of thick and thin paint will be the result. The way to defeat this is to pull away from the surface so that a wider cone of paint is landing, but at the same time the paint to air ratio must be increased to keep the paint wet on landing, to avoid a gritty finish. A second coat, at right-angles to the first, will help to reduce the effect.

COLOUR

Your first problem is finding the correct colours – assuming you know what the correct colour should be. Invariably, when I am giving a talk or demonstration, someone will take up the issue of colour. It is a vast subject. Over the past 150 odd years of steam and diesel (or electric) locomotive paint, technology has changed, pigment sources have changed, original paints have faded, weathered and aged, different works of the same company used different paint-mixing formulae, different foremen in the same works used different formulae, different manufacturers use different formulae. External influences such as light levels, surface reflection, cleanliness, size, surface shape, distance, etc, all affect the way we see the colour.

Take, for example, LNER Green. Now would that be Doncaster Green or Darlington Green, or Stratford Green or Gorton Green or Inverurie Green or Cowlairs Green? Or would it be a Monday morning Green or a Friday-nearly-knock-

This Scale Seven model, running on the correct Irish gauge, was built from the MMS kit by Mike Edge. The blue paint was provided by the customer. The actual blue used by the GNRI is a bit of an enigma, as no one seems to be able to define it. I have, over the years, used four or five different hues including the actual paint used on the preserved locos. The model is painted as running in service rather than as preserved. The preserved engine is missing its tender frame lining.

The lining on the front of the cab that runs down over the splasher top can be done with a straight transfer or, as here, with offset compasses.

ing-off-time Green or a We're-a-bit-short-of-pigment-today Green? I have been told, by someone who knows, that different sides of the same locomotive could be different colours.

However, I have also been told, by someone else who knows, that the LNER, and the GNR before it, both used the same paint manufacturer and the green colour was particularly consistent from its introduction in the 19th century until nationalisation in 1948. The same green, from the same manufacturer, is still used on National Collection locomotives.

Drummond Green of the LSWR is very similar to GNR/LNER green. Is it in fact the same? Similarly, Maunsell's 'Dark' Olive Green is extremely close to GWR/BR Chrome Green but, as the former usually had black and white lining and the latter orange and black (or unlined), they look different.

Take a look at a painting of a locomotive and examine how the artist has painted the boiler. It will be almost white on top and almost black on the underside and various shades in between – so what colour is it? Take a look at your car when it has just been cleaned and consider the reflections off the surface, look at it as an artist would and you will realise that what you are seeing is a multitude of shades and reflection, not just a flat colour. A model of your car would look quite different, no matter how carefully you chose the colour, simply because it is reflecting different things.

We are painting a scale model of the real thing so should we scale colour? Should it be darker or lighter or the same (whatever that is)? Looking at your 4mm scale model locomotive from one metre away is the same as seeing the prototype from 76 metres. Does the intervening atmosphere modify the colour in any way? Should the model reflect this? (Should the model colour fade as it moves away from us on the layout? Sorry, I'm being facetious.) Creating an illusion of distance by using muted

I built this O gauge engine some years ago from the London Road Models kit (now Fourtrack). It has two MSC JH motors, one for each uncoupled axle. The LNWR eschewed their usual black for this engine and Queen Empress on the occasion of Queen Victoria's Jubilee trip to Scotland. Most livery details are given in LNWR Liveries (HMRS), with some additional clues in Carter. Effectively the superstructure is in Post Office red and the remainder in dark blue. The only question mark was the colour of the sand boxes as there is no way of telling from the photographs and the narrative gave no clue. I opted for blue, as they were not lined but I could be completely wrong. The paints used were H19 gloss red and P500 GER blue. The tyres were painted in pale grey, for white. The number plates are by Diane Carney. The lining is particularly complex as it is in gold, edged both sides in blue, with each line a different width. The LNWR coat of arms is by Methfix but the royal ditto was hand painted. Ever complimentary, my friends from the Loco Clinic call it 'James The Red Engine'.

colours on the static scenic effects can be extremely effective but the moving bits should be as close to the prototype as we can make them.

I solve the problem by going to Phoenix-Precision and trusting the wording on the container. These are generally in the right field, although some, I think, are suspect, but that is only a subjective opinion. There are slight differences between batches – just like the prototype.

If you use cellulose paint, for which there is a very limited range of railway colours available – the only ones I know of sold in non-aerosol cans are the Comet Models and Chris Wesson ranges – you will need to match the paint. Again I start from the PP range and take a sample down to my local car paint supplier for him to match. It is a good idea to match a cellulose paint to an existing enamel paint as, invariably, some touching-up will be necessary at some stage during, or after, painting. Cellulose paint can't be brushed on, but a spot of matching enamel will do the trick.

I occasionally need to mix paints to match an existing colour on the model for restoration purposes. The principal problem is assessing the actual colour of the paint to be matched, because of the reflections problem, and comparing it with the mixed colour. The way to do the comparison is to take some black card, cut two similar small holes in it (say half inch square) about a quarter inch apart and use it to view the two colours. The matching colour needs to be painted on a small piece of card and, when dry, placed under one aperture and the other aperture positioned so that the body colour of the model shows through. With the black surround, a true assessment of the match can be made.

It may be that slight adjustment to the shade and hue will be required and that, I'm afraid, is trial and error and time-consuming, as each colour sample will need to dry before a true comparison can be made. As an example, starting from P30 LMS Crimson Lake (one mustard spoon), I had to add 5 drops of black and 9 drops of H70 Brick Red to achieve a match with Bassett-Lowke Crimson.

I have a copy of *Britain's Railway Liveries* by Ernest F. Carter, published in 1952. This contains many colour samples, which are probably as near as one is going to get to the real thing. Mr Carter would have seen for himself many of the pregrouping liveries described in the book so one would assume the samples are in the right field.

Having just read the new *Caledonian Railway Livery* by Jim MacIntosh, there is, in the section headed 'The perception of colour – a cautionary tale', a statement that E. F. Carter thought that the Caledonian Blue looked black on paper so had lightened it! So, a pinch of salt there then. *Caledonian Railway Livery* is an excellent book, a model of how all livery books should appear, yet nowhere is there a colour sample, which shows how difficult it is to be definitive about colour.

The rest of the references in *Britain's Railway Liveries* have to be read with care, as they are a list of contemporary comments gleaned from publications, a number of which are contradictory. Copies of the book are usually to be found at railway book and collectors' fairs, or sometimes on eBay.

The tool I use for matching colours is the piece of black card with two apertures cut out. With it are my samples of green paints which have been sprayed onto glazed white card. Each card has the paint maker, type of paint, date and alleged colour written on the back.

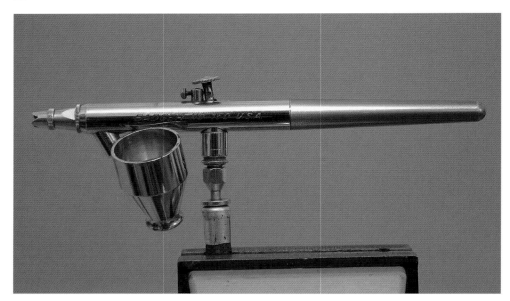

This is my Badger 150 airbrush that I have had for about 20 years. The button on top is pressed down to release the air, which is either on or off; there are no intermediate settings for the air. Pulling the button back moves the internal needle back out of the nozzle, thus releasing the paint. This is variable from a fine mist to a flood. The 7 ml paint cup holds enough thinned enamel for a 4mm scale locomotive. For larger jobs 25 and 50 ml jars are available.

The Badger 200 is a more simple air brush with a single action. Pressing the button on top releases both air and paint in a fixed (but adjustable) proportion. The adjustment is made by moving the internal needle with the screw at the tail end of the instrument. Although the screw can be adjusted when the brush is in use, it is not really practical to do so. This is the type of brush to use where a constant predetermined flow is required. The same paint cup and jars fit this brush.

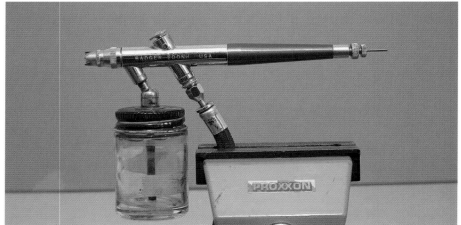

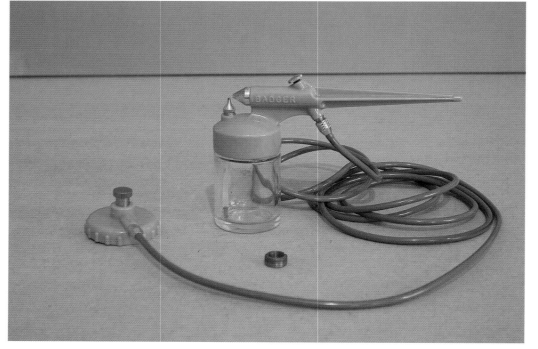

The first paint spray I bought was this model from Badger, and once I had learnt its limitations, and that of the spare tyre for the air supply, I produced some reasonable work, including the painting of Papyrus. This is an external mix spray, which means that it is very easy to clean as no paint goes inside it. The button on top controls the air, which rushes past the bottle nozzle and pulls the paint out of it. The nearer the nozzle to the centre of the air flow, the more paint comes out. The adjustment is awkward as there is usually paint on the nozzle and there is little to grip. What can you expect for a fiver?

PAINTING METHODS

Having chosen the colour, the next problem is how to apply it. There are effectively four methods – air brush, spray gun, aerosol or brush. I use all four.

AIR BRUSHES

Whole books have been written about air brushes and air brushing. Many years ago when I started building models I used a very simple £5.00 paint spray powered with a spare tyre and achieved excellent results. You certainly do not need anything too sophisticated to start with for model railway painting. **What you do need is practice and to learn the limitations of your kit and how it behaves.**

The best way to apply paint is by spraying and, for the modeller, this usually means some form of air brush. The first air brush appeared in the USA in 1879 but the first modern one, to a design we would recognise, was first seen in 1893. The air brush works by forcing air past the head of a tube connected to the paint supply. The action of the air creates a low pressure in the tube, which sucks the paint into the air stream and blows it onto the object being painted.

There are two basic styles of air brush – external or internal mix. The cheapest and least sophisticated is the 'external mix' type where the paint nozzle is in front of and at an angle to the air stream, and is outside the body of the tool. The amount of paint flowing is adjusted by moving the paint nozzle nearer to or further from the air stream; the nearer, the greater the paint-to-air ratio. The atomisation of the paint is not as good in this type as it is in the internal-mix models. The air supply has to be switched off to make the adjustment and usually a pair of pliers is involved. There is no control of the air supply – it is either on or off. This type of kit can be had for under £20 complete with paint jars and hose.

Internal-mix air brushes work on the same principle except that the paint nozzle is in line with the air supply and contained within the body. This makes it neater (but more difficult to clean). There are two types of internal-mix brush – single action and double action. Unlike the external-mix type, the paint supply is regulated by a needle within the paint nozzle – the further it is drawn back, the more paint is released. In the single-action brush, the needle position is controlled by a screw at the back end of the brush and you need to use your other hand or stop spraying to adjust this.

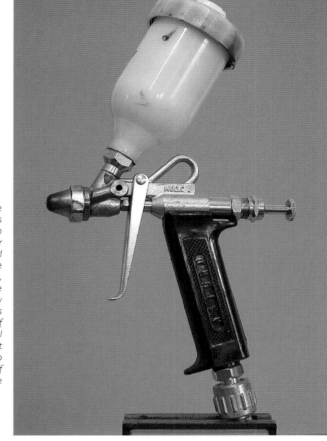

For spraying cellulose paints, I use this Asturo 0.5 spray gun. It works in the same way as an air brush but has a pistol grip and a trigger that controls both the air and paint. The first squeeze of the trigger releases the air and then, the further it is depressed, the paint flow increases. The screw at the tail end is just a means of limiting the maximum flow of paint. This model has a 75 ml gravity feed cup which does get in the way of the sight line, so the aim is different from that of the air brush. As I said, you have to learn to use your kit.

In double-action brushes, the needle is controlled by the same trigger that controls the air, and can be adjusted while spraying. Naturally, the more sophisticated the brush, the higher the cost. I have two air brushes, a Badger 150 double-action and a Badger 200, single-action. The 150 costs between £80 and £100 depending what pieces come in the box while the 200 cost me £30 from Squires. I have painted over 900 models with the 150, so it's done well.

Another thing to consider when choosing an air brush is the size of the paint reservoir. My two Badgers take either a small paint cup, which is sufficient for a 4mm tender locomotive painted with enamels, or larger bottles for larger vehicles and the greater quantity required of cellulose paints. Some air brushes have just a small hole in the top or a tiny cup. Unless these have provision for a larger reservoir to be fitted, they are best avoided for general work.

The article in *Model Railway Journal* No. 159 discusses a number of air brush types

from the point of view of various users. The most commonly available type is the Badger, for which spares come by return of post from Squires, and the most expensive is the superb Iwata. Other makes include Aztek, Paasche and Aerograph DeVilbiss. There are also cheap copies from the Far East but I have no idea if these are worth buying.

SPRAY GUNS

If you are going to use cellulose paints on larger models, a spray gun will be required to deliver the larger quantities of paint required.

Spray guns work on the same principle as air brushes but the general design is different. They usually have a pistol grip and a trigger for regulation. They also have a much larger reservoir for containing the greater quantities of paint required when using cellulose. My own has a 75ml polythene reservoir on top of the gun, gravity fed. The initial squeeze of the trigger starts the air, then further pressure introduces increasing volumes of paint. There is a control at the back end that limits the depression of the trigger, if required.

AIR SUPPLY

Costs do not stop there, though, as there is a source of air to consider. The choices are compressor, air cylinder, aerosol propellant or spare tyre. As compressors are both hobby and commercial items, there is quite a range to choose from. Hobby suppliers are not necessarily the best places to buy a compressor. I bought my first from a well-known model railway shop for about £70. It was small, noisy, did not have a reservoir and only lasted three years. Small silent ones cost about £300 but I bought a small commercial model complete with 25 litre tank for about £160 from the large range on sale at Machine Mart. (That was some years ago – they are much cheaper now!) This has served me well. It is only noisy when recharging and is otherwise silent. If you want a compressor, then identify your needs, take advice and shop around.

Small compressors can only deliver a small quantity of air at their working pressure and therefore may not be suitable for pushing out high volumes of air or even moderate volumes for prolonged periods. Ideally, your compressor should be capable of delivering more air than you need, so that it is not working at its limit. Also you may wish to use it on something bigger one day. When buying a compressor, check that the type you want has the capacity to deliver the volume of air required, especially if needed for grit blasting.

'Must haves' for the compressor are a delivery air pressure gauge, a moisture trap and a reservoir. If not already fitted, the gauge and trap will set you back about £25. A reservoir is needed to take out the pulses given to the air by the compressor vibrations and will also trap the moisture. A long delivery tube may damp down pressure pulses in the absence of the reservoir.

Some compressors are designed to power air tools and these deliver oil in the air in order to lubricate the tools. As we do not want oil in the paint, it is important that you specify an oil-free delivery.

An air cylinder is a convenient silent way of powering the air brush but it depends, of course, on the proximity of a suitable supplier such as British Oxygen, Air Products or a local scuba diving shop. You will also need the right adaptors to connect the bottle to the brush and, of course, a regulator to govern the pressure.

In my experience aerosol propellants are to be avoided at all costs. When my first compressor died I was forced to use a can to finish off painting a 0 gauge coach. The pressure would not stay constant as the can kept freezing up; it lasted for about five minutes and was very expensive. Never again!

The cheapest form of supply is the spare tyre – it must be on a wheel and not just an inner tube, as these have virtually no pressure in them. Badger do an adaptor, which fits into the aerosol connector of their cheaper sprays and enables the air brush to be connected to a tyre valve. One fill of the tyre would be enough to do a couple of coats on a 4mm engine before the pressure gets too low, but you must always be aware that the pressure is falling. Fill the tyre at the garage on the way home or get some exercise with the foot pump.

AEROSOL PAINT

The other principal paint type is the aerosol car paint, which, if you can match the colour, is a satisfactory way to paint your model. The technique for applying the paint has been discussed under 'Primers' above. Car paints these days tend to be acrylic (but with cellulose type thinners) and can be used on plastics with a suitable primer. I find that Halfords Satin Black is just the job for black parts. A few of the paints that have been recommended to me are – LMS Crimson – Rover Damask Red or Ford Burgundy Red, BR/GWR Green, SR Dark Olive – Land Rover Deep Bronze Green, GNR(I) Blue – Ford Wedgwood Blue, LBSC Umber – Rover Mexican Brown, NSR Madder Lake – Ford Lacquer Red. Apart from the Deep Bronze Green, which other professionals and I use, I make no comment on the accuracy of the colour match.

There are some railway colours in aerosol cans available from PP, Railmatch, (both enamel), Just Like The Real Thing and Model-Locomecca (both cellulose). I have never used any of these products so I am not in a position to advise. I have, however, heard many comments on their use, both pro and anti. All I can say is practise, sort out your techniques and never ever use them on your model without first having learnt how to use them.

BRUSH PAINTING WITH ENAMEL PAINT

I habitually use a spray to do the main areas of the model and then, particularly on 4mm and sub 4mm models, brush in smaller areas of a second colour, usually the black. However, it is possible to brush paint the entire model if you are not in a position to spray it. The cleaning process is the same but, as the model will be held in the hand for a far longer time, during the painting process, it is essential that a glove be worn. An additional problem is that the wet paint on the model is exposed for much longer than one that has been sprayed, so that far more dust, dandruff and airborne creatures can land on it. Be vigilant.

It is possible to brush paint etching primer if it is suitably dilute but it needs to be put on quickly and very thinly. If you opt out of etching primer then it's a case of painting directly on to the metal with a matt undercoat or even the first coat of your final colour, preferably matted.

Use a good quality long bristle sable or synthetic brush for large plain areas, smaller pointed ones for detail work and second division for wheels, axle boxes and the like. For general brush work, the use of a top quality brush (eg. Winsor and Newton Series 7) is an extravagance, but you still need to go for one of the more expensive ranges from Winsor and Newton or Daler Rowney.

Brushes need to be cared for. If you go around prodding paint into corners you will soon destroy the end of the bristles, so go in carefully and gently.

Thoroughly stir the paint. Always dilute the paint a little. This can be done with white spirit or boiled linseed oil or both. The linseed oil will lengthen the drying time so that the paint can be brushed out well, but do not exceed 10% oil or the paint will take forever to dry. White spirit will dilute the paint but as it evaporates more quickly you will have to work quickly, especially on large areas. You will also have to top up your paint mix occasionally, as the spirit will evaporate from that, too.

Mix the paint and thinning agent in a small container, just enough for the work in hand, as it will not last very long before skinning over. Use a disposable vessel or one that can be cleaned out easily.

Work steadily and try to maintain that wet leading edge. Put fresh paint a little away from existing paint then work it back into the existing before working it forwards to the new edge. This avoids thick paint at the overlaps. Brush the paint lightly at right-angles to the general direction, then again in the preferred direction. On large areas, such as tender sides, work away from the short edge. This will give a shorter wet leading edge, which is easier to maintain. The boiler can be treated as separate sections between each cladding band, if you have left them on. Don't rush it.

Diluted enamel paint will spread easily and dry without brush marks but it will be translucent. Matt and satin paints tend to dry smoother than gloss as the matting agent aids the flow, but they also dry more quickly. The number of coats required will depend on the colour. Two or three with black or dark green, four or five may be needed with crimson. It's a slow process, but if the paint is flowing well, quite therapeutic.

Clean the brush out regularly and often, as you work, to avoid the paint drying on the brush. It is tedious, I know, but it is for the best. On completion of the work, suspend the brush in cellulose thinners, MEK or a brush cleaner so that all the paint at the base of the bristles is cleaned out. When clean, blot out the solution and reform the point on the bristles with spit or neat washing-up liquid, then store it, preferably with its sleeve on.

If there are blemishes, allow the paint to dry completely between coats and rub down any paint ridges before laying on another coat. Brushed paint will take longer to dry than sprayed paint.

BRUSH PAINTING WITH ACRYLIC PAINT

Acrylic paint seems to be very fashionable these days, especially amongst the younger 'modern image' modellers. It is not something I use, but for the purposes of this book I did some comparative trials by painting the equivalent of a 4mm scale tender side in acrylic and enamel.

I found that the acrylic paint did not flow out as well as the enamel and brush marks were difficult to remove despite diluting the paint with thinners. It dries more quickly than enamel so it is essential that you work quickly and that the brush is washed out with water frequently to prevent paint drying in it.

I would not advocate painting large areas by brush with acrylics.

This is Great Northern *after rebuilding by Thompson in what is, effectively, GER livery. There are no photographs that I have found that show the details of the lining because of the difficulties of picking up the red and also because the engine was in this livery during the war years. I assumed that the red lining would be positioned exactly where the white lining was on a green engine. This 00 gauge model was built by Mike Edge from the PDK kit.*

LBSC 39. This 00 gauge LBSC Class H1 is the DJH kit built by Graham Varley. There are no transfers available in 4mm scale, so all the lettering and numbering has to be done by hand using the method described in the text. The monograms were not easy as so much is crammed into a small space. I drew one at a large scale just to see what was going on and how the letters crossed over and under each other.

LBSC 424. This 0 gauge model of the H2 Class was built by Graham Varley from the Gladiator kit. The lining on these engines was gilt, for which my preferred paint is PP Brass, which goes through the pen just like normal paint. The Umber paint is a cellulose that I had mixed to match Cherry Umber, now discontinued. The darker umber border was produced from a 50/50 mix of enamel umber and black, which was brushed on. The monograms, lettering and numbers are by Guilplates.

AIRBRUSHING THE MODEL

ACHIEVING A GOOD FINISH

The best finish is obtained when the paint lands in a fully liquid form and the coating is of sufficient thickness to allow it to flow out to a smooth surface. Too thin a coating and the forces keeping it sticking to the surface will prevent it flowing sideways to even out the peaks and troughs. Too thick and the forces keeping it on the surface will not be strong enough to stop it falling off and forming a run. I call the point where the paint is about to run, the 'instability point' (IP) and the closer you get to it the better the paint finish will be. And that is where the risk lies.

THE VARIABLES

How much sugar do you take in your tea? One would answer that question to the nearest half teaspoonful. However the pedant would say that it depends on the size of the cup, how much the cup is filled, the size of the spoon and whether it is level or heaped. He could go further and cite the type of tea, type of sugar and its grain size. What has this to do with spraying paint, you may ask. Well, it's to do with finding all the variables that can affect a situation and then trying to assign values to them to get the best result. The trouble is that there are lots of variables when it comes to painting with an air brush or spray gun.

This is where you need to experiment to find the right balance that gives you the best finish from your equipment. The problem is that there are no absolute values for any of the following. I have split the variables, listed below, into three groups. The first group is connected to the act of spraying and are interdependent. The second group is concerned with the spraying environment, equipment and paint, and the third is to do with the object being sprayed.

Group 1
Air supply pressure
Paint:air ratio
Paint:thinners ratio (dilution)
Speed of traverse
Spraying distance

Group 2
Room temperature
Paint temperature
Model temperature

Type of thinners
Paint – type
- solvent
- surface finish
- pigment density/colour
- viscosity/age
- manufacturer
Nozzle size

Group 3
Spray pattern
Size of object being sprayed

The list seems pretty daunting, especially if you are approaching it from a position of zero experience. Unfortunately there are no hard and fast rules and a lot of the suitable values that can be assigned to the above are also very subjective, ie. what works for me may not work for you. The first five are the most important.

GROUP 1

AIR PRESSURE

My compressor will deliver from about 120psi down to 1psi, a tyre will give you, say 35psi down. You actually only need a range of about 15 – 25psi for general painting and when you've found the pressure that suits, you may never need to vary it. The pressure you need will depend on the paint dilution. The thinner the paint, the lower the pressure needed to pull it out of the reservoir. If the pressure is too high, the paint can be blown off the model as soon as it has landed. Paint sprayed at a lower pressure is more manageable.

The higher the pressure, the finer the atomisation of the paint. It is a moot point as to whether the droplet size matters in general painting, as there is no difference in surface finish between paint sprayed at a low or high pressure.

In the case of applying extremely dilute paint as a single coat, for example when applying a 'dulling' coat during weathering, it is a good idea to increase the air pressure to increase the atomisation of the paint. This reduces the droplet size to make the very thin coat more even. I use about 40psi to apply soot and dust.

An important point here is that the pressures quoted are measured when the compressor is delivering air. While it is resting, the pressure in the delivery tube can build up to the safety valve setting, which in my case is about 120 psi. When the spray trigger is first depressed, air will initially

be expelled at the higher pressure until it stabilises at the normal set delivery pressure. It is important, therefore, to let the pressure go down by spraying air only and starting the paint when working pressure is reached. In practice, the pressure reduces very quickly but if you've started the paint at the very high pressure, you could end up with an unsightly splat of paint on the model. If you have a single-action airbrush, then point it away from the model while the pressure reduces.

Spraying at high pressure can disturb paint that has already landed on the model. Remember, ocean waves are caused by wind – not an effect we want on the model surface. Flooding paint is very vulnerable to being pushed around by the airflow, so lowering the pressure reduces the risk.

PAINT : AIR RATIO

This is not something that can be quantified; it is more of a feel. A high volume of paint hitting the model can flood it and result in your reaching for the paint stripper. Too low a volume of paint and the job will take hours to do, together with the risk of the paint drying in the air. Somewhere between is a happy medium where the bulk of the painting can be achieved with a fairly high ratio but with a reduction to get into tricky corners without risk of flooding. Aerosol cans have a high paint:air ratio and the technique for using them can be utilised with the air brush – ie move quickly.

Cellulose paints need to be applied at a higher paint:air ratio to avoid their drying out on the way to the model.

PAINT DILUTION

Thinners to paint ratio for gloss enamels is around 1:1 but again this is subjective. Anyway 1:1 is a good starting point; give it a try on your practice piece then adjust to suit. It depends on the thickness of the paint in the can, the air pressure you feel comfortable with, and the colour and the size of the area you are going to spray. Light creams, as on coaches, and reds as on buffer planks and between frames, need to be thicker than the darker colours just to get some sort of cover without flooding.

You need to be careful with satin and dull paints, as too much thinning will result in the sprayed paint becoming matt. Start with the recommended 40:60 thinners:paint and see how you get on. The thicker the paint, the higher the pressure will need to be.

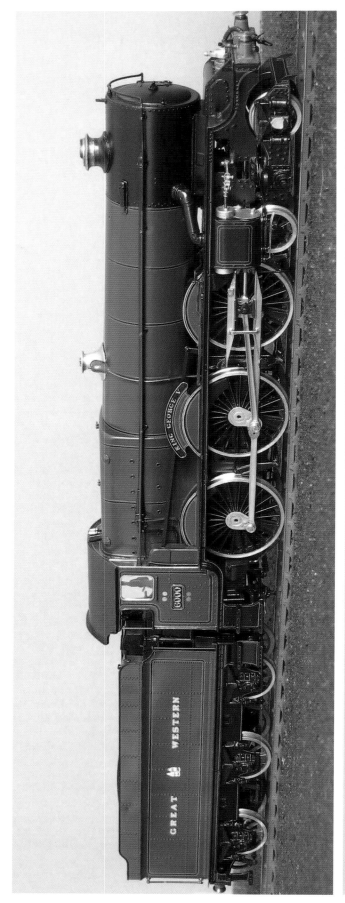

King George V is to 00 Gauge from the Malcolm Mitchell kit, built by Mike Edge and painted in early '30s livery. The pannier is a brass 0 gauge ready-to-run model. The Pontypool Road shed code was made up from CPL transfers.

Whether the model is to be a plain green or black, or a rather more elaborate style, a fine, smooth paint finish is essential.

If you do have problems with orange peel, you can apply your paint in a number of layers of more dilute paint, allowing time for the thinners to evaporate between each coat. The first few coats will be translucent but it will eventually build up to a smooth dense finish. It will take a long time.

Cellulose paints need to be much thinner. A starting point here is 2 or 3:1 thinners to paint. The paint has to be wet on landing but as the thinners evaporate so quickly there is far less danger of forming runs.

SPEED OF TRAVERSE

The speed at which you move the spray across the model is highly critical. The best speed is that where the paint fully covers the area and has sufficient thickness to form an even smooth surface. This is also the point at which, if you are not careful, it could run. I must emphasise that this is where the lighting is so important, so that you can see what is happening on the surface of the paint.

If you move the spray too quickly, you will not get an even coverage in that pass. By repeating the pass, you will build up the paint thickness and eventually you will reach the point where the paint surface evens out. You may feel that this is a safer method but there is a slightly increased risk of orange peel and you will still need to judge how close you are to the instability point.

SPRAYING DISTANCE

The paint must be wet on landing or you will get a poor finish. The wetness will depend on distance, volume and air:paint ratio. I tend to spray with an air brush or spray gun from about 2-3in (50-75 mm) with enamels or cellulose but further away if lightly weathering.

From observation of models at exhibitions, it seems to me that spraying from too great a distance is an extremely common fault. While it feels safer as there is less risk of passing the instability point, the paint finish will be gritty and overly matt.

SUMMARY OF GROUP 1 VARIABLES

High air pressure produces better atomisation but can disturb paint near the instability point. Low pressure is more manageable.

High air:paint ratio gives a thinner but more manageable coating for enamels. It can cause the pre-drying of cellulose and acrylic paints. High paint:air will give a better finish but carries the risk of passing the IP.

Very dilute paint will ultimately give a better surface finish but the risk of passing the IP is very high and so it must be used with high air:paint and low pressure.

The higher the speed of traverse, the lower the risk of passing the IP, but it is less easy to control the aim and spraying distance. Speed of traverse is critical in the approach to IP.

Spraying from a close distance will eliminate the risk of a gritty finish. It will also increase the risk of passing the IP if speed of traverse is too low or paint:air too high. The closer the spray, the smaller the paint cone, so the risk of striping will increase, also more passes will be required to cover the surface.

GROUP 2

TYPE OF THINNERS

The type of thinners used is dictated by the type of paint, as discussed under 'Paint Types'.

The speed of evaporation of the thinners plays a part in the way you spray. If you use a rapid drying thinner (cellulose), the coats of paint can follow each other quite quickly without fear of runs, but the slower-drying varieties such as white spirit require thinner coats with a longer drying time between. 'Longer' can mean just a few minutes. One of the techniques I use is to stop the paint flow but continue with the air, which drives off the thinners and gives the paint a 'surface set'; the trigger can then be pulled back and more paint applied. This is useful in areas that are hard to get at, such as inside the cab. Provided the air is not stopped, there will be no risk of splats of paint on restarting.

I used to use xylene as a thinner for enamel paints, obtained from our local (non-chain) chemists. Supply was not a problem but it had to be ordered. One day I ran out of it, having forgotten to place an order, so I substituted white spirit in the mix. To my amazement, I found practically no difference in application or drying time. White spirit is a good deal safer than xylene so I have continued to use it for thinning enamels.

I have doubts about 'rapid drying thinners' and paint manufacturers' own thinners for their enamel paints. Ordinary bog standard white spirit is a rapid-drying thinner, and it will dilute enamel paint at a fraction of the cost, in my experience anyway.

A practical point. Transfer thinners into small pots for immediate use. The pots should be stable and wide bottomed and clearly labelled – it will wreak havoc on enamel paints if you dip into cellulose thinners when you meant to use white spirit. To reinforce the difference use differently shaped containers.

There are different types of thinners available for cellulose paints. The best is Deep Gloss (also known as Super Flow) thinners and should be used for all spray work. It has a slightly longer drying time, giving the paint time to settle to a flat surface. Less expensive types should only be used for cleaning equipment.

ROOM TEMPERATURE

The room you spray in must be warm, for a number of reasons. Warm paint has a lower viscosity, warm air will hold its moisture better, a warm model will be dryer than a cold one, compressed gases always cool on expanding. Too low a temperature and there will be more free moisture in the air supply, the model surface could be damp and there will be an increased risk of low adhesion.

Cellulose paints must not be sprayed in cold conditions as you can induce a situation known as 'blooming' where the paint dries a milky colour. This is due to minute droplets of atmospheric water condensing into the cold paint.

PAINT TEMPERATURE

Paint viscosity reduces with an increase in temperature; it therefore flows better. The warming of aerosol cans has been described above. After mixing enamel paint and thinners, I often put the paint cup on the room heater while I go and sort out the model and airbrush for spraying. Cellulose paints, after mixing, should always be at least room temperature to avoid blooming.

MODEL TEMPERATURE

The model must be at least as warm as the room you are spraying in. If it is cooler, there is a danger of condensation forming on it.

PAINT TYPE

Paint types have been described above, and the differences between them when it comes to spraying are discussed in detail below under Air Brushing.

SURFACE FINISH

Satin and matt paints are easier to spray as their surface is less reflective so that imperfections are harder to see. The presence of the matting agent seems to reduce the surface tension a little, which will also give a better finish.

Gloss paints are unforgiving and will show any impediments but they dry harder and are the best surface for lining onto.

PIGMENT DENSITY/COLOUR

The density of the pigment will govern the amount of paint needed to produce a uniform colour. This may mean a thicker coat, either as a series of thin coats or one thick one. Whichever way you do it, the risk of blemishes increases. Thin coats mean a longer time spraying and more risk of airborne particles landing, thick coats lead to a risk of runs.

Reds and yellows are the worst, black, greens and blues the best.

PAINT VISCOSITY

Viscosity is not something that can be measured at home but it can be observed by seeing how quickly the paint will run or drip off a spoon. New paints vary from one batch to the next and, once you open the container, the paint will become more viscous with time. Naturally the thicker the paint, the more thinners it will require to produce a sprayable mix. You will get a feel for it with practice.

Modern paints are not as good as those produced twenty years ago. I have some old cans of Cherry and Precision enamel that are in virtually the same condition as they were when I bought them, even though I open them up and use them occasionally. Modern enamel paint skins over and thickens very quickly.

Conversely, cellulose paints virtually last forever. They do thicken up slowly as the thinner evaporates off but all you need to do is top them up and give them a good stir.

PAINT MANUFACTURER

There are differences between the paints produced by the various manufacturers. There may be some chemical differences but the principal ones are pigment density and viscosity. I am not going to be drawn into recommending one manufacturer over another, it's what you get used to – a theme that runs throughout this book.

NOZZLE SIZE

My Badger 150 came with three sizes of nozzle – fine, medium and coarse. The nozzles change the amount of paint delivered for a given setting and also the shape of the paint cone. I almost invariably use the medium nozzle. I used the fine spray for a spell after damaging the medium nozzle and found very little difference at higher volumes but at the lower range a very fine line is possible. I have also used the coarse spray, which will produce a much wider cone at higher volumes but I found it was prone to deposit paint around the nozzle, which, unless cleaned off at quite short intervals, is thrown on to the model in lumps. This is not A Good Thing.

Nozzle size is not a great issue for general painting, you will simply get used to the characteristics of the nozzle you have.

GROUP 3

SPRAYING PATTERN

By 'spraying pattern' I mean the route you travel around the model covering it with paint.

Apart from making sure the paint is wet on landing you also have to maintain a 'wet leading edge' so that fresh paint will always merge invisibly with paint already in place. Doing this on a tender is reasonably simple as you can start at the front edge of one side and, by traversing parallel to that edge, work along that side, around the back and down the other side. Locomotives, with their different shapes, can be problematical.

Take, for example, an ex GWR locomotive in BR Green livery. The green areas are cab sides and front, boiler and fire box, splasher faces and valance (hanging bar in GW parlance) and cab interior. I would start by spraying the cab interior and then continue on the back edge of a cab side and work forwards to complete that cab side; reduce the paint to air ratio, then finish all the cab front; increase the paint, then finish the valance ahead of the cab to the front of the engine; splasher faces one at a time; fire box side with boiler side, slowly rotating the engine so that the paint continues along the top, then down the other side, always maintaining the wet leading edge of paint, not forgetting to take in the front shoulders of the fire box, behind the hand rails and as much of the underside of the boiler as possible. At this point it is probably necessary to turn my hand inside the engine and,

with the boiler paint complete, it will be safe to do so. Having turned it, I complete the valance ahead of the cab on the second side, then the splashers and finally the cab side, ending up at the back edge. The final bit is the underside of the boiler. The wet edge adjacent to the underside of the boiler will have started to dry, but as it's a dark area, possibly masked by the running plates, it is not too critical, so I generally get on and spray it while holding the model on end from the front buffer beam.

A warning note. When the inside of the cab is sprayed, or the inside of a tender, the paint may blow back into your face, so please wear suitable protection for your lungs' and eyes' sake.

Pre 'full yellow end' diesels present the problem of where to start painting, as they are wrap-around green. The answer is to start at a corner, then advance around the model until you get back to where you started.

SIZE OF OBJECT

Working in a larger scale can present problems as, the larger the item, the more difficult it is to maintain a consistent thickness of paint, as it is easy to produce stripes of thick/thin paint or smooth/gritty paint. The use of a high paint to air ratio, putting down plenty of wet paint and working parallel to the shortest edge, will help to maintain a good wet leading edge. The spray should be angled a little towards the edge you are working towards. This will minimise the amount of paint from the trailing edge of the paint cone landing on paint that has started to dry. Practise!

It follows that it is important to construct larger scale models so that they can be broken down into smaller parts for spraying.

SPRAYING ENAMELS

Firstly prepare the painting area by making sure it is clean and free of clutter. You will need the paint, the thinners, a means of measuring them out, something to stir the paint with and a container to do the mixing in. For measuring I use an eye dropper for the thinners and a mustard spoon for the paint, which fortuitously both give roughly the same measure. I had to squash the spoon a little in the vice to make it narrow enough to fit into a tinlet of paint. There are a number of culinary small measuring spoon sets on the market that are ideal for measuring out paint. Choose a set in stainless steel that can be easily wiped clean. I usually mix the paint in the spray cup, which is not the way to do it, but I've not had any problems.

The next job is to check that the air brush is working properly. There's no point mixing the paint yet if the air brush needs cleaning out.

Next, brush any dust off the top of the paint tin, then open it. Check the condition of the paint within. If it is a new can, the paint will need a thorough mixing; I use a paddle made from a piece of brass soldered to a length of 1mm wire that fits into my mini drill which, when set at a low voltage, makes an excellent stirrer. Whatever you do, do not operate the drill at a full 12 volts; I think you can imagine the consequences. Likewise, always hold the can firmly lest it be thrown across the room. If you do not have the luxury of a mechanical stirrer, use a small screwdriver until all the gunge at the bottom of the can has dissipated. If the paint has already been well mixed, give it a short stir anyway.

If the paint has a skin on, it may still be usable but be wary. Cut the skin away in one piece and discard it, then if the liquid paint looks normal it should be ok. Skinning will change the nature of the paint – matt paints become glossier and some pigments may settle out more quickly than others, thus changing the colour balance. If the underlying paint is becoming thick, then bin it and get a fresh tin – unless it is a lining colour, then it may have a second life in that capacity.

The worst condition for a paint is when it is about to form a skin. The surface looks normal but when the stirrer is introduced the surface puckers at first before the stirrer pushes through it. If this happens, on no account use the paint. Put it to one side, with the top off, until a proper skin has formed, which can be removed cleanly.

I measure out the thinners first with the dropper (so that the very narrow outlet of the air brush cup is not clogged with neat paint), then the paint with the spoon. The spoon is immediately cleaned on a paper towel and the dropper popped back onto its bottle. The paint and thinners are then mixed with the small screwdriver, which is also then cleaned. Next I turn on the compressor and check that the air brush trigger is working smoothly. Then I attach the cup, test the spray and replace the air brush on its stand until I am ready to start.

I then put a disposable latex glove on my left hand and then take the primed model from its dust-free drying place (I use upturned salad drawers from an old fridge) and check very closely for glass fibres (again!) and other bits on the paint surface, turn on the fan, pick up the model, brush the surface with a half inch paint brush, spray off the thinners in the cup spout directly into the fan, then, when the paint comes through, I'm ready. I then close off the paint, spray air at the model to drive off any dust and then open up slowly to deliver the mist coat. This is followed seamlessly by the wet coat, in the manner described above.

If you make a mistake at this stage do not panic, some errors are recoverable at this stage whilst others are best left until the paint is dry. If there is a run or a foreign body on the paint on a discrete area of the model, eg a cab side, the area can be wiped clean with a lint-free cloth, dampened with white spirit, then resprayed immediately. If it occurs on a boiler, then it is best left to dry, then rubbed down and resprayed if necessary. If the model is heavily riveted (most GWR engines), rubbing down may be difficult, so spraying with much thinner paint in two or three coats is a safer solution, but of course this will take two or three days to achieve (patience).

While painting, it is sometimes beneficial to close off the paint and continue spraying just air to drive off the thinners. This will allow a further coat of paint to be applied without fear of runs. This is particularly useful when painting in tight corners.

Painting with enamels is quite a leisurely experience, gently filling up areas with paint then moving on, refining the corners, opening up on the larger areas and continuing to apply wet on wet until the colour density is correct and constant.

SPRAYING CELLULOSE

It is quite possible to spray cellulose with an airbrush if you have a large enough reservoir, but the better tool is the spray gun.

I generally thin the paint with four parts 'Superflow' thinners to one part of paint. Because of the greater quantities, measuring with a mustard spoon and eye dropper would take all day, so I use a larger spoon or 1 oz preserve jars, gleaned from hotel dining rooms. I have plenty of paper towels at hand to protect the work surface and clean all the containers afterwards.

The essential thing to remember about cellulose is that it dries within seconds so it has little time to flow out to a smooth surface, which is why it is sprayed in a much more dilute form. There is no limit to the amount it can be thinned – very thin paint will give you a good finish but it will take time to apply layer upon layer to build up the required density of colour.

I use quite a low pressure, generally 12 – 15 psi (0.8–1.0 bar) as I find it much more controllable. With very dilute paint an even lower pressure will be sufficient. A danger is that with a lot of liquid paint around, a high pressure can disturb it so that it dries in a series of waves.

Start with a mist coat to check on shadows and to get the feel of the spray gun, and if you don't spray regularly, this is the time to practise your aim. Now, if you are confident, you move into the next stage, which is the thug spraying. You have to put down lots of paint to get the beautiful surface finish that cellulose gives, and to avoid gritty areas. As I wrote earlier, it is a high risk strategy, but it pays.

Again deal with the detail before the general – the front of side and saddle tanks, front of cab and firebox shoulders, all around dome and chimney. Then follow with the rest in a series of bursts, starting and stopping off the edge of the model. You have to move at a measured pace to deliver the correct amount of paint and the only way you can discover what that pace is, is to be well practised beforehand.

Having sprayed the model, let it become touch dry so that you can pick it up to examine it closely. You may find that there are areas where the paint is thin. The common places are at the top edge of the valance, where it joins the footplate, step plates just under a step, and internal corners. Some times the paint may draw away from external corners leaving thin paint along an edge. These can be rectified by reverting to a mist coat on the affected areas, building up a denser layer of paint and then followed by another flood coat to smooth everything out.

Another way of dealing with thin paint on an internal corner, is to lower the pressure to about 5 psi (0.3 bar) and gently fill it up.

A particular danger area, when spraying with cellulose, is the front of the cab above the firebox. It is very prone to gritty paint so, whatever you do to get paint to cover the area, always finish with a flood coat.

Cellulose is touch dry very quickly but that does not mean that it is fully cured. It can be rubbed down after about twenty minutes, but I would recommend not applying any masking for at least two hours.

If blemishes appear in the paint while spraying, they are best attended to after the paint has cured. Dust particles can easily be rubbed down with wet 1200 grade abrasive. If the rubbing down is light, you don't necessarily have to repaint. A light spray of pure thinner will bring back the gloss, or you can leave it and let the varnish do the job.

Paint runs are more difficult to deal with, especially if they occur on a surface that is heavily riveted. The run can be rubbed down but the danger is that you will rub down the adjacent area at the same time, so

you end up with the same profile but thinner paint. Use a narrow piece of abrasive and try to target the peak of the run.

Heavy runs will mean stripping back the paint on the whole panel. If the paint is still drying, it may be possible to wipe it off with thinners without disturbing the underlaying etching printer but you have to be quick getting the thinners off and light with the touch. If you have used a simple aerosol primer, it will probably come off with the paint and you will need to start again from bare metal.

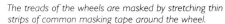

The treads of the wheels are masked by stretching thin strips of common masking tape around the wheel.

If the wheels can not be removed from the chassis, it's a case of 'mask what you can, spray what you can' and brush the rest.

SPRAYING ACRYLIC

Acrylic paints are a relatively modern addition to the painter's repertoire, having first appeared in the 1950s. Their general behaviour is closer to cellulose paint than enamel in that they dry very quickly, but not quite as quickly as cellulose. They also have the drawback of not being able to be removed from a painted surface once they have dried.

The spraying technique is more akin to enamel than cellulose due to the lower dilution giving a denser covering in fewer coats. Because the paint is more viscous, orange peel can be a problem so a higher pressure is required to give a fine enough atomisation. Try around 40 psi (3 bar) for starters, and see how it goes. A more expensive option is to buy a very high quality air brush, like the Iwata, which should give a better atomisation.

The Railmatch range of paints, as I write this, is to become all acrylic and PP are introducing a parallel range of acrylics. The RM range does not feature any gloss finish paint but the PP range will.

PAINTING WHEELS

If you intend painting the wheels after the chassis has been tested, it would be wise to mark each wheel and axle so that, after painting, the wheels are returned to the correct location and orientation.

Wheels take a fair bit of rough handling during construction and running, so it pays to take a bit of care when painting the tyres. The bright nickel tyres of Romford/Markits and Ultrascale 4mm scale wheels have an aversion to paint, so preparation is important. Steel or iron tyres used by Gibson, Sharman, AGH, Walsall and Slater's take paint readily.

Firstly, clean the face of the tyre with thinners to remove any grease and oil. Next thoroughly abrade them with emery or a fibreglass brush. An option at this stage is to chemically blacken the tyre face with Birchwood Casey Gun Blue or similar equivalent. This makes chipped paint less visible. For chemical blackening to work and give an even coat, the metal must be thoroughly clean. I rub on phosphoric acid flux with a cotton bud, wipe it dry and then apply the Gun Blue with another cotton bud, rubbing in well. I normally blacken the back of the tyres of bogie and tender wheels as well – the real ones were never shiny.

Next take some ordinary masking tape, measure out a length just greater than the circumference of the largest wheel, stick it down onto your cutting mat and then cut strips that are equal in width to that of wheel tread plus flange. Wrap each piece tightly around the wheel tread so that it stretches over the flange, and then tear off any surplus. Also, if crankpins cannot be removed, mask them with a bit of tape.

Wheels, especially the small ones, are very light, so the blast of paint is likely to send them to the other side of the room. You will need to stick them down to your painting surface with Blu-tack or double-sided tape. Keep them close together.

Whatever you stick them onto, you will need to be able to turn it as you spray and also store it, with wheels attached, between coats.

Start with the etching primer on the face of the tyres, balance weights and the brass centre of Slater's wheels. Leave for 24 hours.

The procedure for laying on the main colour, whether using an aerosol or airbrush, is similar. Spray from a low angle – 30-45° so that your first pass covers the inside of the rims on the far side and varying bits of spokes. Turn the painting surface through 90° and repeat. This will cover the next arc of rim and some more spokes. Turn and repeat twice more. You should now have painted all of the rims, and the spokes should have received enough paint from the four directions to cover them completely.

If the wheels are a colour other than black, remove the tread masking before brushing the black paint on the face of the tyres. If the wheels have lining, this needs to be done before the second colour is applied. If the wheels have unpainted tyre faces, you will either need to mask them with Maskol or similar equivalent before painting, or prime and paint as usual but scrape off the primer before painting, then scrape off the paint. Both methods are tedious. If choosing the latter method, do not use etching primer.

Wheels can, of course, be completely brush painted. If choosing this method, use an old brush and try to set up a systematic method of doing it. It will be quicker, it will calm you down and the brush will last longer. I do it by painting one side only of the spokes, as the wheel is rotated, making sure that the paint also covers the 'V' at the boss. I then do the other side of all the spokes. This process will have covered the sides and visible front edge of the spokes and most of the rim. I then touch in the remaining bits of rim, tyre and boss. The process of painting the spokes may have deposited blobs of paint on the tyre; it is best that these are cleaned off before applying any further paint to the rim.

PAINTING THE CHASSIS

The completed chassis is a complex structure with moving parts and probably an electric motor. It is sometimes difficult to know the best time to start applying paint as you don't want to start unsoldering electrical connections, nor do you want to cover the motor in paint. Painting too soon may present further problems later on in the build. The optimum time depends on the type of wheel you are using and the type of suspension system.

If using self-quartering wheels, the time to paint is when the chassis has been tested for free running, without motor, but with pick–up points mounted. Remove the wheels and axles, taking care to mark them as outlined above, mask off the areas that will need to take solder, then paint it. Whether you have the brakes and their linkages on at this stage is up to you. They could be added later and brush painted. I try to mount the brakes so that they can be removed, which makes it easier to take off the wheels. You could have all the wiring in place before painting, just mask off the ends that will be soldered to the motor.

If you are using push-on wheels such as Sharman, Ultrascale or Gibson, the chassis should be painted, or at least the area behind the wheels, before the wheels go on. Once this type of wheel is in place and quartered they should not be removed. Alternatively

The green bits are green (cellulose Deep Bronze Green) and the chassis is, well, a dirty chassis colour. Just the black parts to do after suitable masking.

devise a keeper plate system so that the wheel/axle assembly can be removed without wrecking the quartering. This has much to commend it both for future maintenance and for painting the chassis much later in the construction sequence.

As mentioned before under Planning, outside cylinders and associated crosshead guides and valve gear should be designed to be demountable.

On the prototype, inside valve gear was invariably painted to some extent. It is probably better to paint the individual rods before assembly, as they can be a pig to do once in situ. The presence of inside valve gear will make the painting of the inside face of the frames more difficult unless you can drop the crank axle and its associated rods via a keeper plate.

Most railways painted some part of the inside face of the frames in some shade of red, or some other colour, usually between smokebox saddle and firebox front. The remainder was usually black inside. If this is to be a feature of your engine, you should prime the frames in grey and mask off the relevant parts of the inside face before spraying the rest. This will leave a nice grey undercoat to take a bright red. However, the GWR used 'Venetian Red' for the inside face of the frames and some of the valve rods. This is a posh name for red oxide primer.

Some kits of engines with double frames, and tenders without sub-frames, are a problem when it comes to painting, as the wheels may not be removable. I get them through my paint shop at intervals. I mask off as much as I can, spray as much as I can and brush in the remainder.

As the chassis does not get worn through handling, the easiest and quickest way to paint it is with aerosol paints and Halford's, or similar, satin black. Painting the black on with an airbrush takes much longer.

MASKING

Masking has two functions. One is to prevent paint from landing where it is not wanted, and the second is to define a boundary between two different colours or between a painted area and bare metal.

MASKING TAPE

For defining a boundary, you will need a good low-tack tape, not the 'common' masking tape from DIY stores. There are a number of types available but I favour Tamiya, which you should find in model shops that stock Tamiya plastic kits, or model tool suppliers, such as Squires, from exhibitions or mail order. It is not particularly cheap so its use can be minimised by using it only for boundaries and covering the area in between with newspaper stuck to the boundary tape with 'common' masking tape.

Other types of masking are the liquid rubber, such as 'Maskol' from Humbrol,

'frisket film', which is a transparent adhesive film, commonly used for covering library book dust jackets, cling film and many other materials you might think of and put to use.

The first colour to be sprayed does not generally need any masking. The common exceptions to this are as follows:

- Certain situations when spraying cellulose, where the paint is likely to fly past the area being sprayed and landing on a part further away with a gritty finish.
- Spraying the darker of two colours first, for example on a coach side where the second colour is known not to be a good coverer.
- Areas that will be left as bare metal, (brass parts, hand rails, etc.).

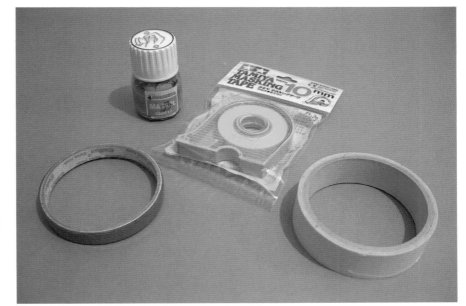

I think that the Tamiya masking tape is the best available, quite tacky but not as vicious as the common masking tape shown below right. The red Cellux tape is also available as a masking tape. It has a very gentle tack, almost too gentle, and the adhesive sometimes has a habit of staying behind when the tape is removed. Maskol is useful for small areas and filling in gaps between taped areas.

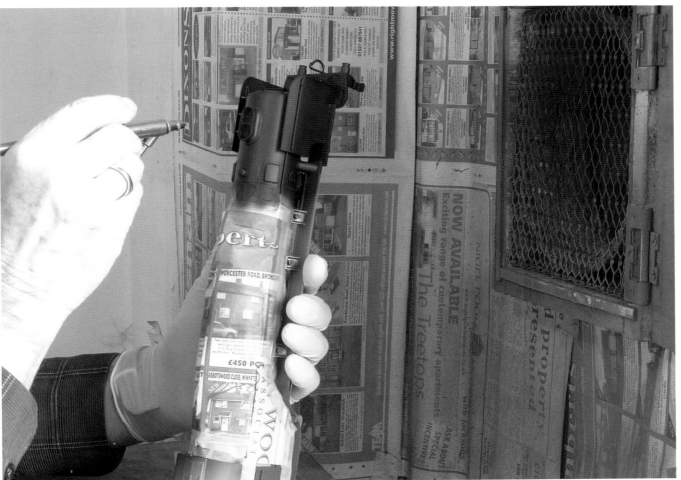

On day 1 the engine and tender were sprayed in LNER Doncaster Green, in this case PP gloss enamel. On day 2 the boiler was masked off in order to spray the smoke box and front end of the footplate in black (H No. 85). I haven't bothered to mask off the front buffer beam; this will receive a brushed-on light grey undercoat (H No. 1) before receiving two or three coats of red. The cab roof was sprayed in black immediately after the smokebox and also the underside of the footplate, behind the buffer plank and footsteps. On day 3 the remainder of the top of the footplate will be brushed in. This will take at least two coats – I usually apply the second after the lining out and black borders have been applied.

It is sometimes possible to spray a second colour without masking. The fronts and tops of tenders are quite easy to do provided you choose the correct angle to aim the spray and the spray cone is not too wide. This is not to be recommended with aerosol sprays. If you wrap the boiler in cling film, it is possible to spray cab roofs without further masking. You should be aware, though, that sprayed paint can go around corners. The turbulence created as the air flows past a corner or body feature can carry the paint on to areas you may have considered to be protected, so, be aware.

Beware of cutting tape that has already been fixed in position – if you nick the paint in the vicinity of the tape you will create a weak spot, so that the peeling tape will lift the paint with it; then you are back to square one. If you need to fit tape between fixed points, use two pieces of tape, starting from each end and overlapping a little in the middle; it is much easier and quicker than trying to measure and cut precisely.

The footplate angle and splasher faces of this Duchess have been painted in crimson lake and now masked off so that the remainder can be sprayed black. This is a case where it is much more simple to paint when the model can be split down into smaller parts.

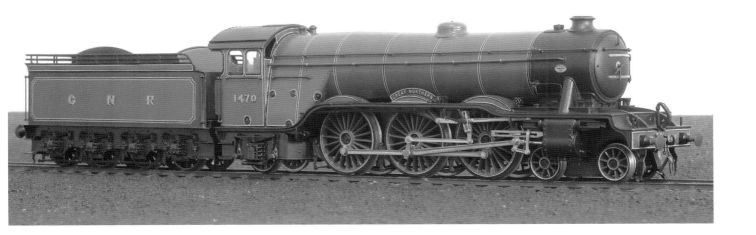

The original Great Northern. The GNR livery is one of the more complex, being a four-colour livery. The brown frame and valances were painted first and then masked. Next the cab roof, smoke box and front of engine were sprayed black and masked. Only then was the main body colour sprayed on. The tender top and interior were then sprayed; normally I do this without masking but I wanted to include the coal rails, so the top of the tender sides were masked. All the white, black and red lining followed, together with a dark green line ruled adjacent to the tender lining. Finally, the dark green outside the lining was brushed on, together with the remaining black bits. It took about twelve days in all. The transfers are the Methfix LNER sheet, the 'G' being fashioned from an 'O'. The model, in 00 gauge, was built by Graham Varley for TMS Models.

A DJH Duke of Gloucester *built by Mike Edge. My American customer for this locomotive likes to have all the copper work polished. This was done by masking with Maskol as far as possible, and scraping the remainder. The train nameboard is the 'Mid-day Scot', one of 71000's regular turns.*

Smooth coach sides are the worst for masking, as any failure in paint adhesion will result in some of the paint coming off with the masking and the whole side having to be stripped and repainted.

An important point about masking coaches is that when spraying the darker colour below the windows, the inside of the windows must also be masked. If you don't, paint will fly up inside the coach, through the far windows and land behind the masking on the other side.

Panelled coaches are the worst for paint leakage under the edge of the masking. This leads me on to the next point – if you are using enamel paints, strip off the masking tape as soon as the spraying is complete.

There are four reasons for this:

1. You can tackle any leakage immediately by wiping it off or lifting it with a brush;
2. It softens the edge of the second colour, avoiding a hard ridge;
3. If the paint dries across the joint between tape and body, the build-up of paint in this area may well be stronger than the adhesion of the paint and so it will peel off;
4. If any fibres are stuck to the edge of the tape as you apply it, and you didn't notice, they will be removed with the tape and not become embedded in the paint;

When removing masking tape, do not pull at it at right-angles to the paint surface. Lift the first bit then fold it over and pull it parallel to the surface; this will reduce the stress on the paint surface.

As cellulose paint dries so quickly, it may as well be left on until the paint is dry,

which is only a few minutes anyway. With acrylics you have a short time in which to tackle under spray so get the tape off as soon as possible and, armed with a water-damp cotton bud, rub away any errant paint.

LIQUID MASKING

Small items, such as whistles, polished brass work, etc, can be masked with 'Maskol' or similar equivalents. Maskol is a rubber solution that is applied by brush (a third division brush). It stays where it is put and forms good boundaries. It dries in a couple of minutes and can then be sprayed over. It is best removed within three days, as then it starts to break down, becoming sticky and will not pull off in one piece. Brushes used in its application must be cleaned in cellulose thinners. The shelf life of Maskol, in my experience, is about six months after initial opening.

Liquid masking should be left in place until the paint has dried, especially if it has been in place for some time.

FRISKET FILM

Frisket film is a transparent sticky-backed film, commonly used to cover the dust jackets of library books. It comes on rolls of various sizes.

My first use was when I was asked to restore some model buses for the London Transport Museum. The models, to 1:8 scale, had been built for the British Empire Exhibition of 1924 by LT apprentices, and so were historic items in their own right. The adverts on the sides were of a patriotic nature (perhaps we could do with more of that nowadays) as befitted the time and the occasion, but at some time, possibly in the 50s, the adverts had been covered over with

more topical subjects painted onto paper and pasted on.

My job was to remove the paper adverts and restore the originals underneath. The paper came off easily enough but took a fair amount of the original paint with it. There was sufficient left for me to trace the outline of the lettering and match the paint colours. Once that was done, I threatened the remaining paint with a chisel and it all fell off the aluminium panels.

When the panel had been rubbed down, cleaned, primed and painted with the back-ground colour, I turned my attention to the lettering. At that time I had only recently become full time in this painting lark and my experience was virtually all in 4mm scale, so the learning curve was somewhat steep.

The film comes with a backing paper that has to be unpeeled as it is stuck to whatever is being covered. This means that the tracing paper needed to be stuck down well to a flat surface to avoid it becoming entangled. Kitchen worktops and sticky tape accomplished that. The film was care-fully unrolled and stuck to the tracing paper without creases. I then, with extreme care, cut around the outline of the lettering with a sharp scalpel, trying not to cut through the tracing paper or damage Her worktop. The difficult bit was the sharp curves around the tops of some of the letters, these coming out somewhat angular.

It was very difficult removing the film from the tracing paper, not because it was stuck fast, but, because of the shape of letters, there were peninsulas of film, eg. the middle of n's and m's, that had to be unpicked very carefully to avoid being torn off. The whole film was then transferred to the panel, making sure it was centred correctly, and carefully stuck down again without creases. The middles of a's, e's, o's and b's etc. were then retrieved and stuck on as accurately as possible.

Once I was satisfied that all was stuck down as well as possible, I sprayed on the main lettering colour and then removed the film after about an hour. Leakages were attended to by lifting with a damp brush and mis-shapes were modified by brush filling or lifting. Once dry, shading and highlights were added as necessary and the final corrections made to the letter shapes. The results can be seen in the photographs.

If you can make or obtain an actual size photograph or drawing of lettering this is a useful technique for private owner wagons, containers, advertisements on shops or hoardings, etc. If you fancy a graffito on the side of your EWS HTA or MBA, photograph a real one, print it scale size, trace it and make a mask from film. Finish off with brushed-in shading and highlights.

Because of the difficulty of cutting the film accurately, it is only a first stage in getting shapes right; all your correcting skills will be needed for a first-rate product.

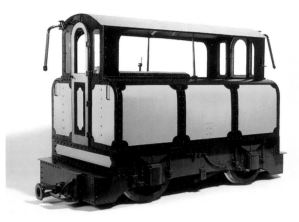

This unusual engine was the first electric locomotive for a tube line. The model was built for the London Transport Museum by Ken Cottle and is to 7¼ gauge. The first colour to go on was the yellow, which was then masked off ready for the black. The lining, which in this scale is about 1 mm wide, straddled the masking line quite happily.

London General Type NS. The painting of the advertisements on this bus, and three others, is described in the text. The work I had to do on this bus was to copy the 'Buy Australian Apples' and 'Buy Empire Goods' advertisements, together with some touching up. The LT red, by the way was an exact match with H19, Gloss Red. The size of it can be judged from the Workmate it is standing on and the size of the concrete blocks in my garage wall.

A Midland Railway Kirtley Goods constructed from the Slater's kit in 7mm scale. Painting this engine was complicated by the fact that when I received it the external springs had already been soldered in place. I had to unsolder them and then devise a method of fixing after painting. This is where a bit of planning comes in. Of course, a livery like this presents many challenges to the novice and some aspects of it were a little daunting for me, too. The splashers were lined with centre compasses after the engine body had been fitted into my frame, with the little reverse curves above the footplate being finished by brush. As much of the remainder as possible was lined using offset compasses, including the rim of the dome. In this situation it pays to make sure the edge of the dome is properly formed so that a clean line can be drawn from it. All the black paint (H85) of the engine was applied by brush because of the complications of masking off the red parts. Likewise, the wheels and cranks had to be brush painted, as they could not be demounted from the chassis. Although it is an ex-works engine, I did paint the brasswork with a spot of very dilute black to give a more scale sheen to the parts and to bring out the relief.

CHAPTER FIVE
LINING LOCOMOTIVES

There are two common styles of lining for locomotives – edge lining and inset lining. There is also a third style, which is the horizontal stripe, used on streamlined or 'air-smoothed' engines.

Edge lining is where each panel has a fairly wide band of colour, typically between 1in – 3in (25 – 75 mm) and usually a dark colour, separated from the main colour by a thin line of a lighter colour 1/8in–1/2in wide (3 – 12 mm). The Southern, LMS and LNER used this style wherever the engine was lined and the GWR used it on splashers and cab fronts. Where frames were lined, it was invariably edge lining.

In the inset style, the lining is set in from the edge about 5 or 6in (150 mm) but follows the general shape of the edge. The GWR and BR used this style and the LNER also used it on tenders together with edge lining.

A number of pregrouping companies used both styles together, notably the North Eastern Railway. A good reason for not modelling that railway is the amount of lining on the engines.

There are a number of methods of lining engines. These are:

Commercial transfers, rub-down or
    waterslide
DIY Transfers
Bow pen
Tubular pen
Brush

WATERSLIDE TRANSFER LINING

Tools required – small cheap paint brush, scale rule, straight edge, curved-blade scalpel, dividers or pencil and paper, paper towel, decal softening solution.

Transfer lining is very popular as it requires no draughting skills but it has the drawback of depending on the manufacturer's perception of what is acceptable lining. The product's accuracy depends not just on aesthetics and scale accuracy but production issues and robustness. My philosophy for lining is that it should be subtle and to overall scale dimensions. All the transfer lining I have seen on the market tends to be too bright and the lines overscale in width, so much so that some 4mm scale lining can be used for 7mm to good effect.

The best transfer lining is for LMS crimson locomotives, where the prototype straw or yellow lining was up to half an inch wide against the black border. The lining for SR engines and LNER tank engines is a close second as this was a single white or yellow line with a black border. The worst is a tie between the GWR/BR orange/black/orange and the LNWR/BR red/black/grey. The former should, of course, be orange/green/black/green/orange and the latter red/black/cream/grey. You might get away with it in 2mm but the cream line should be visible in 4mm and it shouts at you in 7mm.

Transfers can be successfully used for simple coach lining, as these, too, were fairly wide lines on the prototype.

I have to admit that I have never tried Pressfix rub-down transfers although, on the first engine I ever built, a K's Bulldog, I used Kingsprint rub-down for the tender because that was the only type available at the time that gave me the right shape for the coal plates.

Anyway, there are a number of waterslide transfers on the market, the most usual being by Fox Transfers. They offer a generic lining sheet for each of the Big Four plus BR and also custom lining sheets for a growing range of locomotive classes, generally to match the ready-to-run range. A small range is produced by Guilplates for LBSC (Stroudley and Marsh) in 7mm only.

Successful application of waterslide lining depends on taking time to set out lining positions and cutting accurately to length and width. A rectangle on a tender side needs two long pieces exactly the same length and two shorter pieces ditto, plus the four corners. One problem with the transfers is that sometimes the line widths are not constant so that there is an abrupt change of width where a straight meets the curved corner. This can be rectified, once the transfers have set, with judicious use of a fine paintbrush to overlay paint on the lining to reduce apparent width, or increase it, as the case may be. Just slapping the lining on and not bothering to make corrections is sloppy work.

A strategy for putting the rectangle, with curved corners, onto a tender side would be to cut the four straights, a little over length, and the four corners and put them in a dry saucer or shallow container. Set a pair of dividers to the distance from the bottom edge of the tender to the lower line of colour. (You will have previously worked out what the distance should be for your livery option.) With tweezers lift out the transfer for the lower line, lay it flat on the model adjacent to where it is to go, and then wet it with a brush. An alternative is to dunk it in water first, but you may find that it curls up and ties itself in a knot. Any surplus water should be removed when it is on the model. While it is soaking, move it so that it is as close as possible to its final position, so that, as soon as it is ready to be pushed off the backing paper, it can be moved by the shortest route into position. Now check, with the dividers, that it is the correct distance from the edge and, by lifting the tender to eye level and looking along the line, that it is truly straight.

Repeat the process for the remaining edges, resetting the dividers as appropriate. It is important that parallel lines are actually parallel to each other, and that the right-angles are true. This takes precedence over the line being parallel to a dodgy edge.

Next, position the first corner dry, to assess whether anything needs to be cut off the length of the adjacent straight transfer. Cutting transfers should be done with a curved-blade scalpel (Swann Morton No. 10), by gently rocking the blade across the transfer so as not to damage the underlying paint. The corners could be laid so as to overlap the straight, but this will result in a patch of visibly brighter colour. If I were doing it, I would want them to butt up, cutting through both layers and removing the surplus. The lower transfer can be re-wetted to soften it for lifting away.

With transfers you have only a limited time in which to apply them and work on them to get them positioned properly, so it pays to get everything that you may need collected and at hand.

The Fox Transfers custom lining sheets contain complete panels of lining for the specific locomotive cab and tender/tank sides. It would be folly to try to apply these in the one piece as there will simply be too much to do in trying to get the four edges all aligned at the same time. If one line of a parallel pair passes over more rivets than the other, it can end up shorter than its mate. The transfers can also stretch when wet. The best solution is to cut them up into

This is a typical Fox Transfers 7mm scale specific transfer sheet, in this instance of BR lining for an ex LMS Patriot. Many other types in 4 & 7mm scales are available. This one commendably has a gap between the orange and black lines, and overall the scale width is correct, but the black line is missing from the valance lining and I think the corner radius on the panels is too small.

more manageable sections. However, as the sections of transfer are the correct length, your setting out and application need to be very precise because you no longer have the freedom of overlapping to adjust the position of the corners.

To place the lining on a tender side, I would cut the panel into four pieces – the two verticals with the corners attached, cut just beyond the tangent points so that there is a millimetre or so of horizontal straight attached, and the two long horizontal straight pieces. Place the first vertical using a set-square and dividers to put it precisely where it should go; take your time over this and keep checking it. Next lay on the lower horizontal piece so that it butts up to the corner and, again with dividers, check its distance from the base of the tender all along its length. Now you have this basic 'L', checked and viewed from all angles, and if you are satisfied you can go on to the next stage. You will have to work quickly now, as the final three joints will have to be made before the remaining transfers dry out. If there is a difference in length between the long straights at this stage, the still-wet vertical could be tweaked a little to close a gap on the one edge while creating a small overlap on the other. It is important that the vertical component stays vertical – you can't just lean it over a bit.

As the adhesive may take some time to harden off, the transfers are vulnerable, so do no further work on that side until you are sure it can be handled and can be turned over to do the other side.

When the transfers on both sides are set, carefully tweak the joins by overpainting in body colour or lining colour as necessary to maintain a constant line width around the corners.

Minimise your use of water. If there are any bubbles of water on or around the transfer film they will dilute the adhesive. Mop up surplus water, leaving just enough to make the transfers workable.

A major problem with waterslide lining is the presence of rivets on the model. Two of the Big Four were especially fond of snap-head rivets (GWR & LMS), with Peppercorn of the LNER a little way behind, but catching up. If the lining runs over a line of closely spaced rivets, you are in trouble; if it just crosses a line of rivets, or encounters an occasional rivet, the situation is retrievable.

DECAL SOFTENERS

This is where we need to discuss decal softening solutions. There are a number of types on the market but the most commonly used seems to be Microsol from the US company Microscale and the equivalent

from Humbrol. This is used extensively by the model aircraft fraternity. It needs to be used with care as it acts by softening the paint and varnish from which the transfer is produced. Once softened, the paint film has no strength so it can be distorted irretrievably with the slightest touch. Be warned.

To bed your lining transfer down over rivets, first brush a little of your preferred solution over the rivets, position the lining transfer and then brush more solution on top. After a minute or so, very gently and carefully, apply pressure on the lining with the brush so that it sits down into the valleys between the rivets. Should there be any distortion, you will need to tweak the lining back into position with a wet cocktail stick or the end of the brush. The process may need to be repeated after drying.

On some models the rivets are well over scale and make the job of lining, by whatever means, very difficult. Would it have been possible, at the planning stage, to assess this and modify the rivets? In extreme cases they could be filed or cut off. Lets face it, which looks worse on the finished model – distorted lining or the odd missing rivet?

If the lining simply refuses to sit down over the rivets, a solution is to carefully cut out the offending portion and paint the, hopefully short, section of lining in with a fine brush – after carefully matching the colour.

RUB-DOWN TRANSFERS

Tools required – Scale rule, straight edge, curved-blade scalpel, stylus (from plastic sprue, soft pencil, cocktail stick rounded at one end), dividers or pencil and paper.

The most common are the range of 'Pressfix' transfers by the Historical Model Railway Society (HMRS), which covers BR and the 'Big Four' plus SR Spam-cans and Pullmans. The same provisos as waterslide transfers apply in regard to the accuracy of some lining.

In use, the section of lining is cut from the backing sheet, placed in position, sticky side down, then transferred by rubbing the backing paper with a stylus. When all is stuck down, the backing paper is wetted with water and then lifted away. That's the theory at least.

In practice, the backing paper is a little too opaque to see exactly where the lining is and once it's stuck it is difficult to lift and move. A solution to this is to use diluted methylated spirit (1:3, water:meths). This can be used to render the backing paper transparent so that you can see what you are doing and enables you to get a brush under the lining so that it can be moved around a little to attain a perfect alignment. Do not use neat meths as this will fetch the paint off.

The method of setting out is the same as for the waterslide type.

LINING WITH A BOW PEN

Tools required – Bow pen, spring bow compasses, dividers, fine best quality brush, cocktail sticks, gloss paint, white spirit, scale rule, substantial straight edge with polished edge, small square, templates if required, plastic card scraps.

This is the method I use. It is the *only way* that fine, near scale lining can be produced in the smaller scales.

Availability

The main stumbling block to the method is the acquisition of a draughtsman's bow pen (also known as a ruling pen). Their use in the drawing office has been superseded by first the tubular pen (Rotring) and then the computer-driven plotter. As demand fell, the principal suppliers of bow pens disappeared from the market. Thornton, Kern and Wild have been gone for some time, Staedtler recently, leaving, as far as I know, only Jakar, Ecobra and Haff as the principal manufacturers. There may be others but I have no experience of them. The first named has a reasonable availability from graphic arts shops provided you can explain to the young assistant what it is you are talking about so that he can locate it in

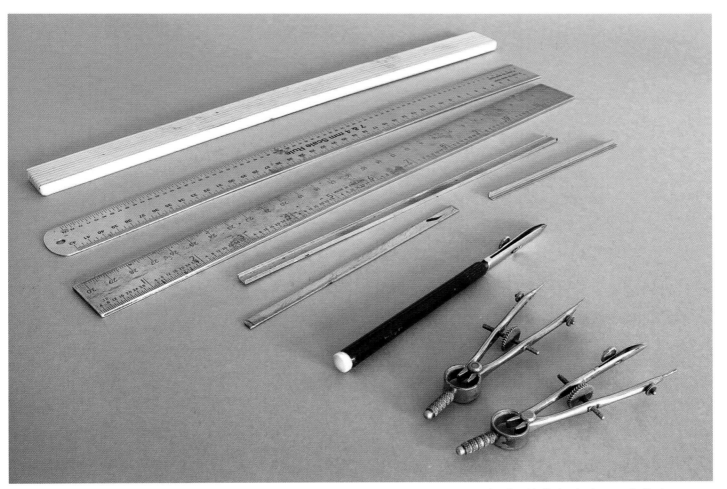

These are my essential lining tools. At the front are the compasses and dividers, which are part of my student set – the best I could afford at the time – and still going strong. They are British made, by Thornton. Next is my usual pen, this is a Haff 135H with hardened tips. The pieces of brass strip, channel and angle are all out of the scrap box. I have other, shorter pieces that see occasional use in situations where longer straight edges won't fit. The angle is useful to slip over a rivet edge when using offset compasses. My general ruler was part of an adjustable square; it is heavy and chunky so that it has plenty of inertia, giving it stability. I keep the edges polished so that the pen runs smoothly against it. The scale rule is by CPL, one of a number they make in various scales. This one has both 4 and 7mm, which covers 95% of my work. The length of wood strip is a rest and is useful if I am working over wet paint. I simply hold one end and the other rests on the bench, on the model itself or on a prop of some sort.

Fig. I – THE BOW PEN TIP

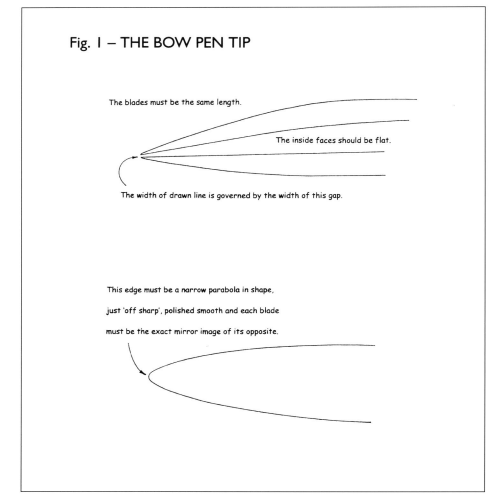

The blades must be the same length.

The inside faces should be flat.

The width of drawn line is governed by the width of this gap.

This edge must be a narrow parabola in shape,

just 'off sharp', polished smooth and each blade

must be the exact mirror image of its opposite.

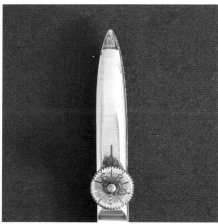

The Haff 135 bow pen that I use for all my ruling work. I like its short strong blades that stay in position relative to each other when held against the ruler or other lining guide. Longer, more whippy blades can close up and stop the paint flow when pressed against the lining guide.

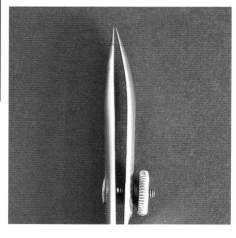

the relevant catalogue. The problem is that when you get it home you will find that it won't work because, as a third division pen, in my opinion, what you have bought is an instrument that has to have its tip ground to a suitable shape and smoothness to enable it to function. Similarly the Ecobra is a second division pen and will generally require some honing.

The best pens, in my experience, are made by Haff, who make a number of different types, together with spring bow compasses. Visit *www.haff.com*.

You may already have a pen in a drawing set of your own, or inherited, which may or may not work. They can all be made to work, as they are fairly simple tools and just need a bit of TLC. Here's how. The principle is that the paint or ink runs between the two blades and exits from the narrow gap at the end on to the work piece. The width of line to be drawn is governed by the gap between the blades at the tip and is adjusted by a screw connecting the blades together. A good pen will draw a line so fine as to be hardly visible and up to a maximum of about 0.5 mm. One fill of the pen with paint of the right consistency will line out a complete 4mm scale panelled coach side.

Preparing the pen

Each blade must be the mirror image of its opposite, flat on the inside and a sharp parabola on the outside, both broadside and sideways on. Each blade must be the same length. The tip should be just off sharp so as not to cut the paint you are drawing onto. The gap between the blades should taper from base to tip.

The best way to hone the pen is with fine emery paper – I use 1200 grade – frequently stopping to examine the points under a magnifying glass and continually testing it when the points are beginning to conform to the description above. I switch to a really worn emery or polishing (crocus) paper at the end to polish it. Once it is there, it should last for years with a little care. Do not touch inside the blades, as a chamfer worn inside the tips will prevent paint flowing.

Using the pen

For lining work we need good lighting to minimise shadows, somewhere clean and quiet to work, not too warm, inner peace, spouse/partner in good mood, and, if required, soothing music. The tools are initially simple, as listed above. I say initially because you will develop your own aids as you improve. My own ruler was once part of an adjustable square, quite thick and with only mild indentations for the graduation marks. I regularly polish the edges.

The technique for using the pen is simple. Set the tips so that there is a small gap, take a cocktail stick, dip it into the well-stirred paint and transfer a drop to the pen, putting it between the blades just away from the tip. Wipe the cocktail stick and any paint from the outside of the pen. The paint will slowly flow down to the tip of the pen and stop. Put the ruler in position, take up the pen, check that the paint is flowing, on a piece of card and check and adjust the line width on a piece of smoothly painted scrap. Then run it alongside the ruler with the gap at the tip parallel to the ruler with just enough pressure to keep it in contact with both the ruler and the lining surface and at a steady speed so that a regular flow is maintained.

Paint consistency

There is no need to thin the paint. The thinnest lines are drawn with a dense gloss paint onto a gloss surface. If you thin the paint it will spread.

The paint should be the same consistency as thick cream. That is not easy to quantify but it should not run off the end of a cocktail stick. It may drip off but you should be able to keep it on the end by rotating the stick between the fingers. This is the test I use to check if the paint is the right viscosity. The idea is that the paint is pulled out of the pen rather than falling out. **If you have to thin normal paint to get the pen to work, then the fault is with the pen.**

Sometimes paint is too thin and so has to be thickened up. If the oils have separated from the pigment, some can be poured off into a secure container and the remaining contents stirred for use. The oil can be used to thin paint that really has gone too thick for use. If the paint has already been mixed, then all you can do is leave the top off for however long is needed for it to thicken up.

If the paint is too thick for use and you haven't any of the decanted oils, a few drops of white spirit will thin it but this is only a temporary measure, as the spirit will evaporate quite quickly. Another method is to add a few drops of linseed oil, but go carefully as too much will render the paint very slow drying.

I find that the 'middle third' of the paint in the can is the best for lining. The top third can be too thin and the bottom too

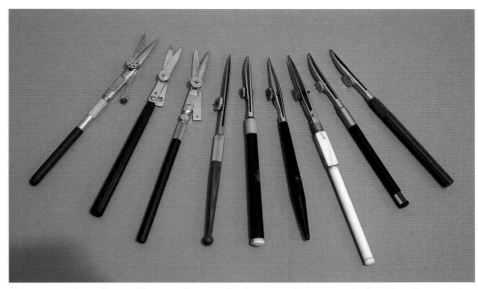

This is some of my collection of bow pens. I'm not really a bow pen junkie, nor an avid collector but if I see one that looks as if it will work, and the price is right… On the left are three 'twist open' pens. These are excellent for cleaning out without changing the setting. The pen in the centre is my Haff 135, to its left is a Haff 133 and right is a Kern. The Haff 133 is advertised as being the finer pen but I prefer the 135 with its shorter, less flexible blades. The bone-handled pen is a Harling with an unusual hinged blade that can be opened right out for cleaning but, unfortunately, it needs a new handle. The two on the right are by Staetdler, cheap and cheerful, which I honed up into decent lining pens.

Fig. 2 – LINE FAULTS

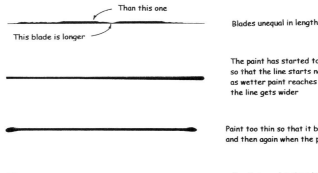

Than this one
This blade is longer
Blades unequal in length

The paint has started to dry at the tip so that the line starts narrow and then, as wetter paint reaches the tip, the line gets wider

Paint too thin so that it blobs when first contact is made and then again when the pen slows at the end

Pen tips need serious inspection and honing

thick. I tend to hang on to tinlets that are nearly empty and use the contents to mix with paint that is too thin, to give me the creamy consistency that I like.

Colours

The paints that I use for lining are generally Humbrol but some, more esoteric colours, are from the PP range, all gloss. I use H5, Dark Admiralty Grey; H7, Buff (for cream or straw); H9, Tan (for orange); H19, Red (for vermilion); H21, White; H22, Black; H69, Yellow; P984 Brass, for gold. If I am using white on a light background such as Adams's Pea Green, I will use it as it is, but against a darker background I will add a little black to tone it down a little. For ochre coach lining I use P625 M&GN Engine

Golden Brown or a 50/50 mix of Tan and Yellow. For red lining on a crimson background I use P994 Buffer Beam Vermilion, which is a dense paint, prone to drying quite quickly if not continually pulled out of the pen.

The smaller the scale, the darker the lining should be, as inevitably the lines will be wider than the scale width. The 2mm scale B12 illustrated on page 52 is a case in point; the white lining has additional black added and the vermilion lining of the tender frames is actually maroon.

A number of articles that I have read have advocated the use of inks for lining. I have never used ink and none of the other professional painters uses ink. Ink is not dense enough. Forget ink.

Featured in the raw in MRJ No. 145 Portfolio, 7mm scale Dartmoor was built by John Edwards using the DJB kit as a starting point, and he also did the authentic weathering. I did the bit in the middle. Adjustments had to be made to the lining positions to cater for slight errors in the kit. The top line on the locomotive is slightly lower than it should be in order to line through with the top line of the tender. The yellow lining on these engines is awkward to do as the yellow paint is so translucent. The way to do it, after carefully setting out the position, is to draw in the outline of the stripes and then let them dry. On day two, fill in with two or three touching lines with a pen set to draw a broad line. Put down plenty of paint, making sure you don't work too near the edge and fill the space up a couple of inches at a time. Don't forget that the lines return around the end of the panelling at the cab entrance.

Photo by JOHN EDWARDS

One of the more daunting tasks is lining a Bulleid Pacific in their Southern livery. In theory it should be straightforward as all the lines are straight. However, there are a number of problems in relation to the setting-out of the lines and also creating a nice dense even line with yellow, which has poor coverage. The engine and tender, with chassis fixed, need to be placed on a true flat surface so that the level of the lines can be set out with a height gauge. You will need to peer closely at photographs to see where the top and middle lines go on your particular engine. You may need to make adjustments to cope with any difference in the relative heights of engine and tender, where your model may differ from the prototype. The top line goes at the top of the tender side and this level has to be transferred to the engine. The middle line runs just below the cab windows and this level has to be transferred to the tender. The bottom line is just above a line of rivets at the bottom of the body side, in practice, about 2 inches above the base of the casing over the driving wheels. This also governs the position of the black border on engine and tender.

I draw in the outline of the stripes on one side and then, on the following day, fill in with three or four thick touching lines. Doing it this way ensures that the edges of the lines are well defined. If the whole width of line were put in at the same time, there is the risk that the paint will slump and spread. In the photograph you can see that the middle stripe outline is in and I am progressing the infill a bit at a time along its length.

Practice

As I said above, practise lining on an old model, or bits of painted metal before trusting yourself with a real model. By all means practise drawing straights and curves on paper but the pen will behave differently on that medium, as it will have a bigger contact area.

You will have to practise holding the pen at a constant angle to the ruler so that the tip is always the same distance from the edge. One of the benefits to an experienced user and disadvantage to the beginner is the degree of freedom you have in the angle of the pen and, therefore, the distance of the drawn line from the ruler. It means that I can draw two parallel lines without moving the ruler but all a beginner can do is get a wavy line because his wrist and fingers were not rigid enough. Drawing a long straight line is a whole upper body movement with forearm, wrist and fingers not moving relative to each other.

Have plenty of space for your pen arm to move into. That side of your table should be clear of obstruction and ideally your forearm or elbow will be supported on a low-friction surface as it slides along.

I lay the model on a piece of clean black A4 size card on a cutting mat to do the lining. If necessary, it is propped up with blocks to keep it stable. This is where I find out the discrepancies in the model and may have to start making compromises.

Setting out the lining

Firstly, I check if the vertical edges of the model are truly perpendicular to the horizontals – quite often they are not – and also, if opposite edges are parallel to each other. If any edge is not straight, or not at right-angles to adjacent edges, I have to choose a datum from which to set out accurate lining.

The datum for a locomotive or tender is usually the edge of the footplate or tank base but it amazes me that so often this fundamental feature of a locomotive becomes a curve, or series of curves, in the model. Not only does this make it more difficult to line the footplate angle but the cab side lining has to be 0° or 90° to this line.

A special case is that of the LNER streamlined A4 with skirts removed, where there is no datum available on the locomotive. In this case, the locomotive must be set up on its chassis and a horizontal pair of dots marked on the cab side using a height gauge. Even if it is an LNER blue

one, with no cab lining, the cab numbers will still need to be parallel to the track.

Another, more extreme, special case is the LMS streamlined Coronation and the Bulleid original Pacific where you need to set up both engine and tender on their

chassis in order to set out a line parallel to the track from the front of the engine to the rear edge of the tender. If there is a mismatch between engine and tender lining, it will jump out at you.

The streamlined Duchesses are not to everyone's liking; Stanier certainly did not like them. This 0 gauge model is from the Tower Models kit built by Graham Varley. Of the two schemes the blue is the easier to paint as it only has twelve lines of colour in the lining on each side — each silver stripe is bordered by a dark blue line. For the silver stripes I used H Aluminium, initially ruled on to form the edges of the stripes and then filled in by brush. The result was a nice even finish to the silver without brush marks. Care has to be taken with the upper of the two narrow stripes as this runs along a line of rivets. Also, because the lower stripe runs over the shoulder of the cladding forward of the cab, it has to be slightly wider than the upper stripe. The 'landmarks' for setting out the stripes are that the top stripe runs just below the cab window, and the base of the bottom stripe just skirts the bottom of the angle iron joining boiler cladding to cab. As mentioned previously, the upper narrow stripe runs through the row of rivets and the lower is in the middle of the gap, bisecting the sand box lids. To set out the tender lining, both engine and tender need to be set up on their chassis and the levels transferred with a height gauge. The positions can be marked with pen and paint or by making a minute scratch in the paintwork with the point of the gauge. The front end stripes are executed with french curves and some dotting in. There is no easy way; do a bit, sit back and look at it, alter it, do a bit more. There are no particular landmarks on the front end that can be used for setting out but there are some good front end photographs in publications.

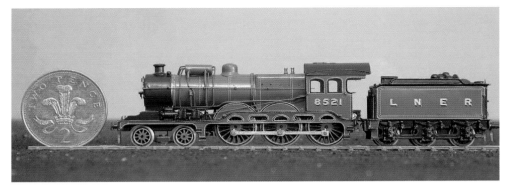

This 2mm finescale B12 (known as a 'hiker' because of all the apparatus on top of the boiler – a feed water heater) was scratch built by two members of the Copenhagen Fields group. No bigger than my thumb, it was quite a challenge to line out. This was only the fourth 2mm steam engine that I have painted, and easily the most complex. The problem with working in this scale is that minor imperfections in the body shape and edge contours, which are not seen from normal viewing distances, can play havoc with a line produced by offsetting.

Edge and inset lining

For edge lining, I set a pair of dividers to the width of the broad band of colour running around the edge, and use them to set up the ruler as I go around the model.

Setting out inset lining is a more difficult problem, as you need to maintain each line parallel to the edge and, also, to the other lines in the group – and at a constant distance apart. I use two pairs of dividers for this work, one for the edge distance and the other for the overall width of the lining. On BR and GWR green liveries this is 2.25in (56mm), which is 0.75mm in 4mm scale. A practical solution, if you have a proper Imperial ruler, is to use 1/32in and work inside the marks on your rule, (1/32in is 0.79mm). Unfortunately) using 1/16in for 7mm scale spacing is a little too wide so the easiest way to do that is to set your Vernier gauge to 1.3mm, then set your dividers to that.

At its smallest practical setting, my bow pen will produce a line a scale $\frac{1}{4}$ inch in 4mm scale.

The other essentials for lining and setting out are spring bow compasses and dividers. You can see that I have removed the point from the compasses and substituted a length of 1mm diameter brass wire for use in offset work. The wire does not need to extend much beyond the length of the pen.

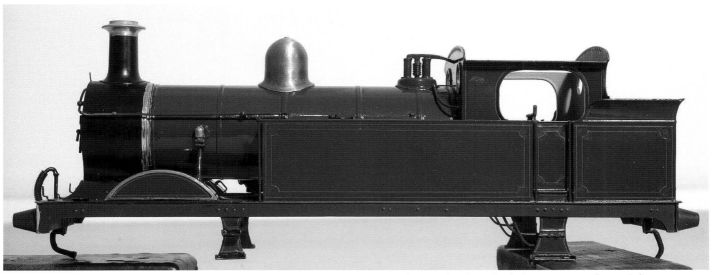

The first colour of lining, in the case of Wainwright's SECR livery, is the red, as it is the closest to the edge and is the key to setting out the remainder.

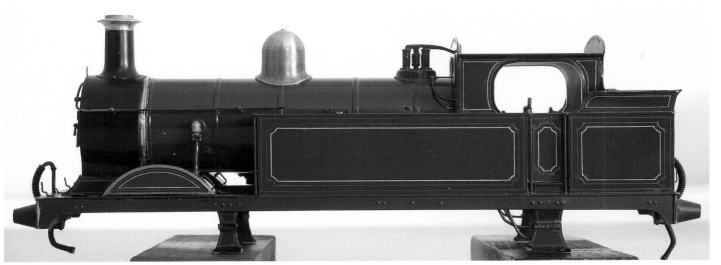

The next is the yellow ...

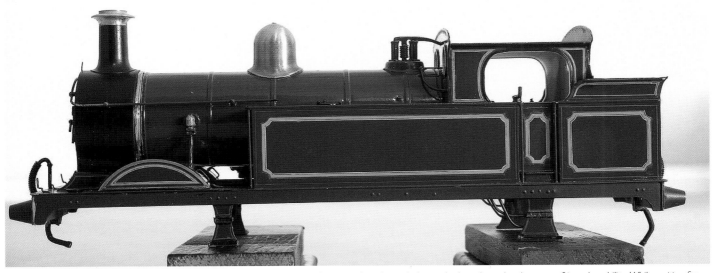

... which is followed by the light green infill. Notice that there is not yet any lining on the valance. I always do the valance last because of its vulnerability. While waiting for paint to dry on the body, the chassis and wheels can be done.

John Brighton's SE&CR Class H in 4mm scale. The lettering is a transfer by Kirtley Models, the brass number is from a Martin Finney GWR etch, but virtually correct. The garter and shields are hand painted.

This and the LBSC Stroudley livery must be the most ornate general service livery of any locomotive in the world. The style was a product of the affluence and confidence of Edwardian Britain. This engine came to me in postwar Southern black, which I had the pleasure of stripping. For the livery details, I copied the perserved engine and found that translating the livery to the model was reasonably straightforward, except that there was so much of it. There are five colours on the tender axle boxes, for example. Every spoke on the engine is lined, and joined to the next spoke by a half loop at the boss. The main difficulty was lining the angle iron that joins the boiler cladding to the front of the cab and top of the splashers. It twists and turns this way and that, yet still has to have one edge lined in red, the other in yellow, and light green in between.

LINING WITH A TUBULAR PEN

The principal tubular pen on the market is the R L Moore Master Lining Pen, which Bob Moore demonstrates at many exhibitions up and down the country. The pen has three sizes of nozzle available, the smallest of which is 0.22 mm in diameter. This is equivalent to 2/3 inch in 4mm scale and just over 1/3 inch in 7mm. The other sizes are 0.34 mm (1in & 0.58in) and 0.5 mm (1.5in & 0.85in) There are two guides available to give offsets for drawing lines adjacent to an edge, the one gives a zero offset for drawing a line on the edge and the other is a 1/32in offset (2.4in & 1.4in). These guides can be tweaked a little to give alternative offsets. It is a simple matter to make guides from scrap brass and wire to slip on to the pen for other offsets.

The tube pen is designed to be used with fresh H or PP gloss paint that has been well stirred, and warmed to reduce the surface tension. Should the paint be a little too viscous to run, a drop of Ronson lighter fluid can be added – other types are not as good. Fill the reservoir by transferring the paint on a screwdriver tip or pipette (use a drinking straw), then, to get it started, gently blow the paint through until a drop appears at the tip. It is then ready for use.

Because the paint dries out at the tip while the pen is not in use, it is best to have your work well planned so that pauses are minimised. If the pen is to be put down for a few minutes while something else is being sorted it would be prudent to keep it running by starting it every so often on a piece of scrap. If you do need to stop, the pen must be emptied and cleaned, as the small bore tube can quite easily clog with dried paint.

Lining with the tubular pen is not dissimilar to using a bow pen as very little pressure is applied. Gravity will keep it in contact with the surface and a little gentle pressure is required to keep it in contact with the ruler or template, especially when working around the outside of a curve.

The pen comes into its own in the larger, model engineering, scales where the line widths achievable equate to scale widths. In gauge 1, for example, 0.22 mm equates to a little over 1/4 inch.

With the tube pen, more use is made of templates than with the bow pen; this is because no compasses are available and offsetting is limited by the number of guides available, or that you have made yourself.

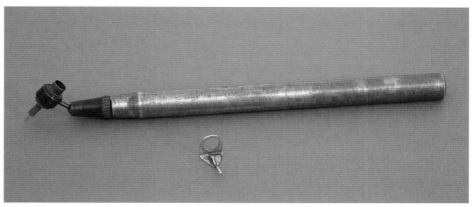

The R.L. Moore 'Master Lining Pen' is available with three sizes of tip and two offset guides. The guide shown is one I made for this picture, just to show how easy it is.

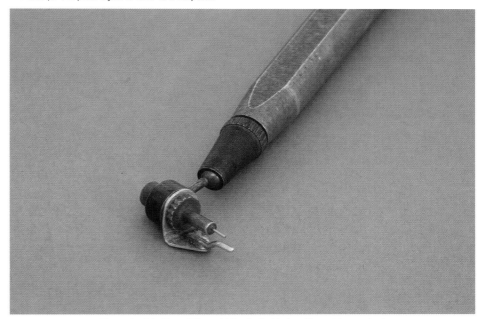

This is the R.L. Moore 'Master Lining Pen' with the offset guide attached.

CORRECTING LINING ERRORS

Before we proceed further, it is time to deal with correction techniques. If you know that mistakes can be easily rectified during the lining process you can approach it with much more confidence. Lining is not always straightforward, even for the practised expert. Putting in corners by brush often leads to differing line widths. Imperfections in the surface and lining over rivets often induce local blobs. As a beginner, your lining will have many problems.

The most common error is to start a line with a slight thickening as the pen first makes contact, and finishing with another thickening as you slow down and stop before lifting the pen off the work piece. This can be minimised by using thicker paint so that when the pen stops, so does the paint.

To rectify lining by removing unwanted paint, you will need a good brush with a fine point and bristles that nestle well together, this is to give a strong capillary action. Dip the brush into clean white spirit, then blot out most of the spirit onto absorbent paper – a paper towel or a piece of newspaper. Use a cheap variety of paper towel as the 'ultra absorbent' types, and paper handkerchiefs, have loose fibres in them. With the damp brush you can gently stroke the side of a line to reduce its width – what is happening here is that some of the paint is sucked into the brush but some is pushed back into the line. You can also

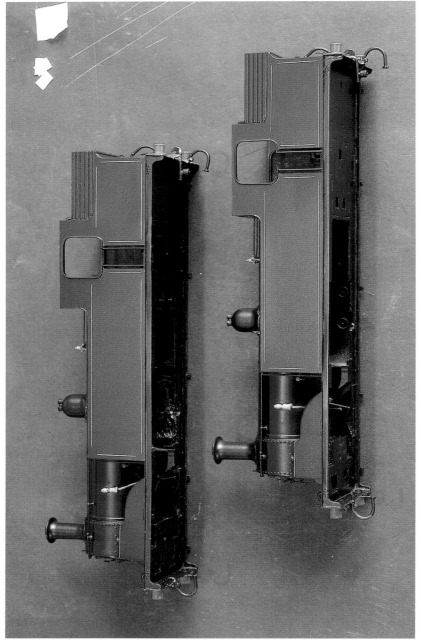

A pair of M7s underway. The majority of the lines are straight on the M7, so I start with them. These are the cream lines, the ones that are so often missed out.

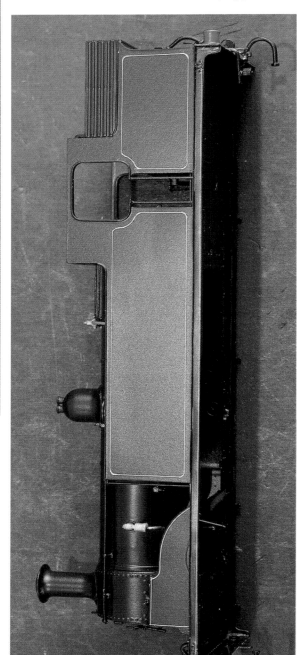

The splasher curve is drawn by offsetting with the compasses and the remainder with a fine brush. This is the first raw attempt, with no tidying up.

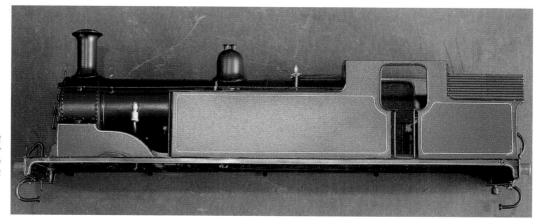

All the curves are now corrected by lifting unwanted paint and carefully applying new paint where necessary. This will now need to be put away for 24 hours while the paint dries off.

brush over the top of the paint to remove it completely. While doing either of these things, the brush must be cleaned and blotted frequently or else you will just start to spread the paint around. With this method paint can actually be pushed back into line, especially useful when tidying up rounded corners. Ideally, these correction techniques will be used after the paint has dried off a bit so that it is lifted more cleanly.

If the base paint is matt, this method is less successful as the matt paint is absorbent and so it will be more difficult to lift the surplus paint, but also some of the thinned paint you are lifting off will soak into the paint around the area you are working in. With a gloss base, the paint can be lifted more cleanly and any that is spread around can be rubbed off when dry with a dry cloth.

Lining paint can be removed very successfully when just dry by brushing a little white spirit over it, then pushing it off with a cocktail stick. With this method there is no spread of dilute paint and no marks are left.

It is important that you have enough time available to complete the task. You are bound to use paint-lifting techniques and, as I said above, they are best done after the paint has gone off a bit. Enamel lining paints can be lifted quite successfully and cleanly, even after 24 hours. So if you only have a short time in which to work, you must make sure you can get back to it within 24 hours. There's no point sneaking in to the modelling room to put in half an hour's lining then going away for a long weekend.

If you have made a gross error and need to lift all the lining, simply dip your paper towel into the white spirit, squeeze off the surplus, then wipe off the lining. You can do this with a cotton bud if you are not lifting too much paint, but be aware that wisps of cotton can stick to adjacent wet paint.

DRAWING CURVES

The real problems come with having to draw curves. I employ a number of techniques depending on the radius and shape of the curve, and where it occurs on the model. There are five methods:

(1) using a brush
(2) using a template with the pen
(3) using compasses to draw a circular arc
(4) using compasses to follow an edge
(5) using a straight edge or a rest, and 'dotting in'.

DRAWING CURVES WITH A BRUSH

For this it is important that the very best quality of fine-tipped brush is used. I use Winsor and Newton Series 7 brushes; 00 is fine enough. The Series 12 miniature brush seems to have disappeared from the market, as it does not appear on the W&N web site. These brushes need to be looked after and only used for fine work. It is so tempting to use them for general brush work, but resist, it will only shorten their life.

When I do the curved corners on lining, I simply join the straight lines with a tiny arc with a brush. In the prototype inset style lining, the radius on the outer curve of a corner is generally about 4in (100 mm) for BR or 3in (75 mm) for GWR, which equate to 1.33 mm and 1 mm on a 4mm scale model, and the inner is just under 2in (50 mm) or 1in (25 mm). I always do the smaller curve first and use it as a guide to brush in the larger to a consistent radius, which is that little bit more difficult. Sometimes when I can't use method (4) for various reasons, I have to do a more complex curve with a brush, for example the curves adjacent to the cab on the BR M7. Sometimes I do it by eye, sometimes I set it out with a series of tiny dots and then join the dots.

The main problem with brushwork is that the paint may go down less densely than with the pen, so that a second coat may be necessary. If that is the case, make sure the first coat is absolutely the right shape before you let it dry. What I some-

'Dotting in' the red line over the coupling rod splasher, using the splasher edge as a guide.

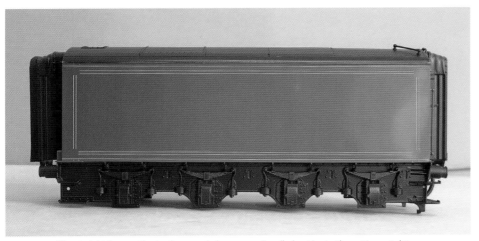

The straight lines on the tender are ruled on conventionally, keeping to the setting-out dots.

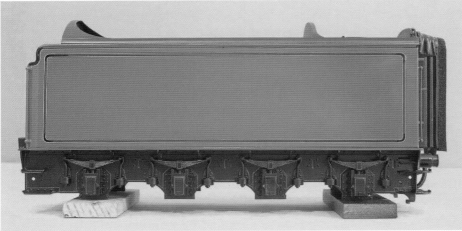

The white corners are brushed in, and on the following day, the black outlines are ruled in and then filled with a brush at the corners and the edges, but with the bow pen between the lines.

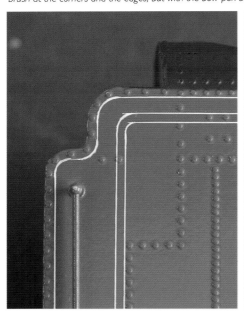
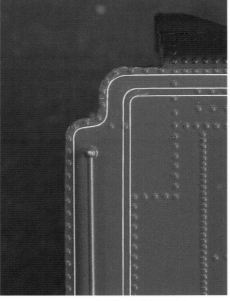

Left: The first stab at the lining on the tender of 520. The white lining is positioned to (generally) avoid the rivets. The straights are ruled in and the corners brushed, giving these raw results – complete with unwanted dust and hairs. Right: The lining has now been tidied up with the white spirit damp brush. The rivets are probably overscale.

times do is pick the paint from between the pen blades with the brush, as this will have already lost some of its solvent and become thicker. Paint taken from the edge of the can, from where a brush was previously wiped, or from a palette, will also be more dense than fresh paint. Another way is to let your brush just touch the surface of the paint in the can so that there is the tiniest drop on the end. This can be brushed out to a millimetre or so but it will be quite dense. This is 'dotting in' with a brush.

Sequence

The sequence for lining an inset panel is to firstly set out the lining using tiny dots of paint measuring in from the edges (after first checking that the various edges are straight and at right-angles to each other). Rule the lines on in pairs (if there are two lines the same colour) so that there is a panel with the corners missing. It will be virtually impossible to draw a line of precisely the correct length, starting and stopping in exactly the right place so do not worry too much about this as it can be corrected.

Set the dividers to the outer radius of a corner. With one point in line with the outer line of one set of lining, mark the wet paint of the line at right-angles to it with the other point. Turn the dividers and repeat for the other side of the corner. What you now have are the 'tangent points', where the straight and curved lines meet. Continue around the panel until all tangent points are marked. Put the model away for an hour or two, or even up to 24 hours.

Cutting back lines

With a cocktail stick, dampened with white spirit, rub the unwanted portions of the lines away. You can do this sooner, with a damp brush, but there is the risk that the wet paint will spread across the surface of the model rather than being simply picked off, which will be a disaster if you are lining onto matt paintwork. Now we have the straight lines of the panel, all of the correct length, with gaps for the corners, all of the correct size.

Adding curves

With the finest first division brush, brush in the first inner corner followed by the adjacent outer corner, taking care to describe a perfect arc and maintain the correct and constant line width. I write

This 00 gauge NER 4-6-4 or 2-Co-2 electric is a Judith Edge kit built by Mike Edge. The prototype was built in 1922 ahead of the proposed electrification of the NER mainline from York to Newcastle. Because of the Grouping, the electrification never happened and No. 13 then spent most of the rest of its life languishing in the Darlington Paint Shop. It was finally scrapped as BR 26600 in 1950. The model presents a number of challenges to the painter. The most difficult part of lining panels is brushing in the curved corners; there are 192 on this engine. The other thing is, of course, the elliptical number panel, which is careful brushwork. The last is that practically everything on the chassis is lined.

this, of course, with tongue in cheek, as you will not be able to do it. Do the best you can and then correct it. You may find that it is easier to do one of the corners than the others. I find a 12 o'clock to 3 o'clock corner the easiest so I tend to turn the model through 90° for each corner.

Incurved corners such as those used by the Lancashire and Yorkshire and Mr. Marsh on the London Brighton and South Coast are a little more complex. The principles are the same, ie. rule the straight lines, cut back the corners, brush in the curves. However, the inside lines of double lining are shorter than the outer. The method of setting this out is shown overleaf.

The two curves at the corner are similar in length so it does not matter which is done first. Study photographs of the prototype to gauge the angle at which the curve meets the straight; it is usually greater than 90°.

Stroudley corners are a particular pain. Here two sharp curves meet at a point on the bisection of the corner. This is also the white line, the brightest of the set, and so has to be right. It can be set out by drawing a short line at 45° to the corner as close as possible to where the two curves meet. After putting in the curves, lift any surplus setting-out line.

When putting in larger radius or complex curves with a brush, it is easier to put down a series of very short strokes, pulling the paint forward as you go. Work with a tiny dab of dense paint on the tip of the brush, recharging frequently. It is more important to get the general line of paint parallel to the edge than it is to get a perfect line. The edges of the line can be tidied up later, but there is no point having a clean line in the wrong place.

Gladstone. Stroudley's LB&SCR livery is not easy. The general run of lining is fairly straightforward but, as you can guess, it's the corners that cause the problems, the buffer beam panel ends being the worst. On all Stroudley engines, the toolbox could be left off to facilitate drawing in the vertical lines on the back of the tender or bunker and also the panels on the ends of the toolbox.

INCURVED CORNERS

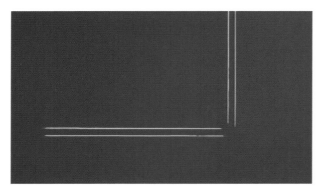

The straight lines are drawn to as near correct length as possible. Being slightly over length is better than too short as it is easier to cut back a line than it is to extend it.

Set your dividers (or mark the edge of a piece of paper with pencil dots) to the scale distance from the corner to the start of the curve. If the actual corner is not marked, then line up one of the divider points (or the pencil dots) with one line and with a sharpened cocktail stick (or the other point of the dividers) make a mark in the wet paint of the other line. Repeat for the other side of the corner, then repeat for all the other corners in the panel.

With a fine brush, just damp with white spirit, lift the paint between the end of the line and the mark.

The inner line of the pair will need to be cut back further. If you were to draw an imaginary line at 50° to the end of the outer line, the point at which it crossed the inner line would be where to make the mark. 50/40 setsquares are as common as hens' teeth so use a 45/45 and leave the line a tad long.

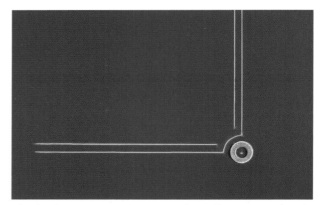

Brush in the outer curve so that it is a circular arc. This is not easy. A good idea is to raid your collection of spare washers and find one you can place centrally on the corner so as to give you a guide as to what a circular curve looks like. Use it as a guide, not as a template. It does not matter initially if you put down a curve that is a bit ragged on its edges so long as it is in the right place. The edges of the line can be corrected by stroking them with a spirit-damp brush.

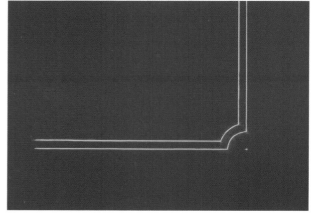

Brush in the inner curve. Use the outer curve as the guide and set your dividers to the line spacing to check the distance between the two curves. Tidy up the edges of the painted line.

A 4mm scale Terrier, more commonly known as 'Rooters' on the Brighton system. It would help enormously if the rear tool box were built separately and fitted after painting as accessibility is hampered by the tall lamp brackets and vacuum pipe. The lettering and numbers still need shading added.

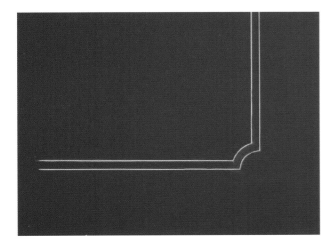

Let the paint dry thoroughly over a couple of days, then take a dry cotton bud and rub off any stray paint marks from the outside of the lines. If there is to be another colour between the lines, the area between them need not be cleaned up. You can relax now as putting in the black paint between the lines is not as difficult. If it is to be SECR Wainwright light green though, it is very prominent and will need much care.

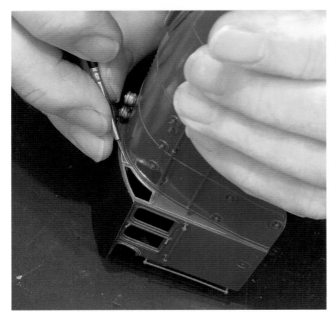

Cab front lining is always a bit of a fiddle if the boiler is permanently fixed in place. The straight line on the lower cab front was done from the edge but the curve on the edge abutting the fire box will be a combination of brush and pen work, using the fire box itself as the template with a suitable spacer made from plastic card.

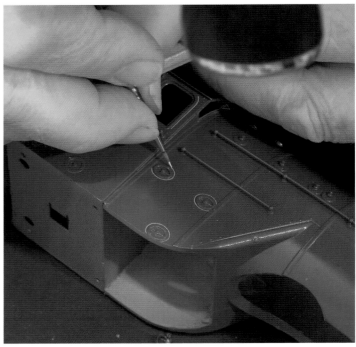

Yet more wash-out plugs.

The cab side with the white lining nearly complete. The lower corners of the cab window lining need rounding off and the lines need to be squeezed in either side of the cinder guard.

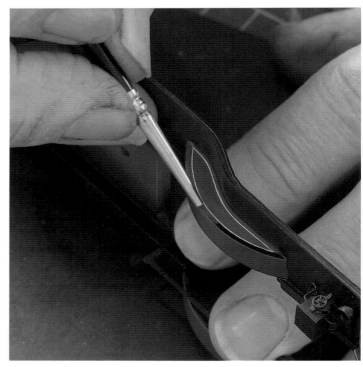

The white lining on the splasher was all done with compasses, the top curve from the edge, and the bottom by closing up the compasses tightly then allowing the point to follow the footplate. The black was simply brushed in – following the outside of a curve is relatively easy.

One of the problems with LNER green engines, with the exception of the North British-built A3s as originally turned out, is the fact that the wash-out plugs in the green areas are lined – and they are either circular or elliptical. You could centre punch the central bolt and use compasses to draw the circular white line, but this one is done with just a fine brush and the surplus paint removed with a white spirit damp brush. The wisps of paint outside the circle will be removed with a cotton bud when dry; on the inside they are left to be covered with the black paint.

The elliptical lining is done in the same way except that you don't have the option of using compasses. Practice and patience.

This 0 gauge A4 is the top of the range Martin Finney kit constructed by Mike Edge to my commission; it even has a working inside cylinder. The livery is an early version of British Railways when locomotives were still being turned out in company colours but with BR numbering and lettering. This one has a Guilplates smoke box number with the early ER non-standard six. The lining is minimal but complex. I followed a good side-on photograph to get it somewhere near right. There were numerous versions on the prototype, depending on who lined it and where it was done. The lower line is in fact straight but it passes over an awkward concave curve at the bottom of the boiler cladding. The line above the handrail is also nearly straight until it curves round to pass behind the chimney. The killer is the curve joining the two bits. This is pure brush work.

DRAWING CURVES WITH A PEN AND TEMPLATE

For curves of a larger radius, say between 3 and 15 mm, again depending on location, you can use a Radius-aid, which is a template used for drawing small diameter circles. The problem with the bow pen is that it has to be turned as you go around the curve, so 3mm radius is about the lower limit, and then you can only successfully do about 90° of the curve before having to turn the model and restart. With a tube pen, which does not have to be turned, the problem is that of keeping the pen in contact with the template at such a small radius. This is where practice comes in! The Radius-aid is useful for arcs adjacent to cab cut-outs and for curved valance drops.

The Radius-aid is less use where, because of its size, it cannot be placed close enough to the work piece, so this is where you have to make your own. If you were truly diligent, you would have made them up in plastic card at the start, from the shapes of the kit before assembly. If repainting a proprietary or finished model, you will have to make templates as best you can. They are particularly useful where the lining is in three dimensions, for example, the front curves of an A4 or cylinder lining. I have a pair of templates in thin aluminium which are shaped and bent to do A4 lining, but as most of the models that come my way have fixed hand rails, they are a bit of a fiddle to use – but you would leave yours

off until later wouldn't you? For other 3D lining situations I have many bits of bent 00 rail and brass. If you do not have bow pen compasses, then templates will be the only answer for some curves.

I have a circle cutter (Olfa), which will cut circles in plastic card from 5mm to

75mm radius. These are available from graphic arts suppliers. The difficulty is in fixing the precise radius as you will need to measure the radius of the adjacent edge, subtract the scale edge distance and further subtract an allowance for the distance between the template and the drawn line.

The setsquare is essential for marking out lettering, and lining where the model itself is not square. Also present is my home-made square with 1in sides for use where there is insufficient space for the larger one. The 'Radius Aid' sees less use now than it did when I was starting out. The type shown here, with the external circles, is more useful than the ones with just internal circles but, unfortunately, less easy to come by. The French curves, which come in sets of three, were devised in the days when Art Nouveau was the height of fashion. They have limited practical application in lining models except for the front of A4s and streamlined Coronations. If you do not have a pair of compasses, they would be more use for doing compound curves in larger scales, or for producing templates for such curves.

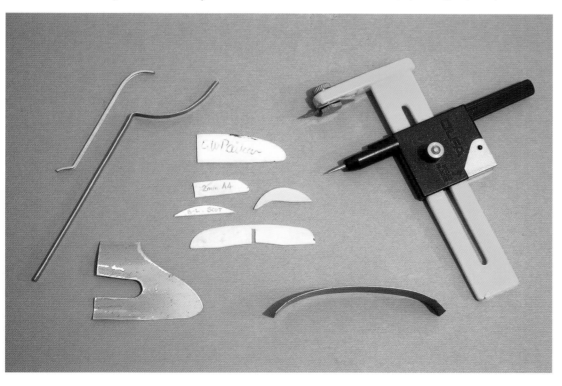

Although I don't use them now, I made up a number of templates in the early years to cater for awkward bits of lining. The plastic templates are for the front end of a GW railcar, a Bassett-Lowke Royal Scot splasher, a 2mm scale A4, another splasher, possibly a 7mm scale GN Atlantic, and the cab front for an engine I can't remember. The metal strips are for lining on a curved base, tops of splashers, boiler bands and, bottom right, the black edge to a GWR coach roof. On the lower left is an aluminium template, one of a pair, for the front end of a 4mm A4. The Olfa circle cutters can be used to cut circular curves in plastic card between 5 and 80mm in radius. They are also useful for cutting out curved transfers, using the same centre as the compasses used to draw them.

This latter will be dependent on the thickness of the template and the angle at which the pen is held.

The curves at the front of the streamlined Coronation Class are theoretically circular when viewed head on, but as they are laid on to another curve, they are a form of ellipse. I use French curves to form the shapes after first setting out various reference dots to work between. On the red engines there are twenty lines on each side, all to be brought to a point above the coupling hook, so it is arguably the most difficult bit of lining one could meet.

I must say that I prefer the red Duchesses despite their being more difficult to line out. On these there are twenty lines of colour each side and the gold does not go on so well as the silver. Both the streamliners have been lettered with HMRS Methfix transfers, which, although the correct shape, do not have the coloured borders to the characters, so these have to be applied separately. You can see from the photograph that I forgot to put the black line in the centre of the '6'. This is another Tower Models kit built by Graham Varley.

The piece of kit I use for holding the loco body when drawing curves from a centre point is shown here. I made it many years ago when I had a proper job, but was only modelling in 4mm scale. The base is a piece of 19mm shutter ply measuring 250×150mm. To make it suitable for 7mm scale work, I have fixed a piece of 6mm MDF to the underside. At one end of the ply I have screwed two pieces of 12mm wide pine. The gap between these takes one of the brass brackets. The brackets are made from some prehistoric frame material, the type that came in K's kits. The brass is $\frac{5}{8}$ in × $\frac{1}{16}$ in or 16mm × 1.6mm and is 100mm long. To one end of each I soldered some smaller section bent into an L with a hole drilled in the short leg to take the body fixing screw. One length of brass is drilled in the middle to clear 8BA to take its fixing bracket, which is made from a piece of scrap. This bracket is drilled to clear 8BA on one leg and slotted to take a wood screw on the other. The plain piece of 16mm brass is bent to a slight curve so that it is a tight fit in the slot between the two bits of pine. To facilitate release from the slot, it has slots filed in the end so that a screwdriver blade can be used to lever it out. The other part of the assembly is the sliding platform, shown upside-down here. Originally it was a plain piece of copperclad about 23mm × 60mm, on the underside of which, are soldered three pairs of 4mm scale copperclad

crossing sleepers. There are three positions to cater for the various sizes of engine that I deal with. The gap between the sleepers is a tight fit around the frame brass, so that it can slide but not wobble. To make the platform fit for 7mm work I screw to it a piece of 10mm thick hardwood. Finally, in the plastic box are the various lengths of 6, 8 and 10BA fixing screws, a couple of small wood screws, washers and other bits and pieces I have had to fabricate over the years to fit the oddballs to the frame.

The holding brackets are fixed to the body of the engine. It does not matter which way around they are. If you are one of those modellers who prides himself on using only a one-screw fixing for the body, you cannot use this method – unless you are prepared to drill and tap a second hole.

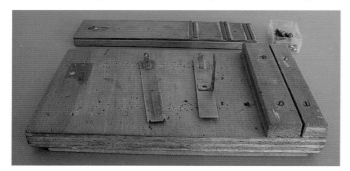

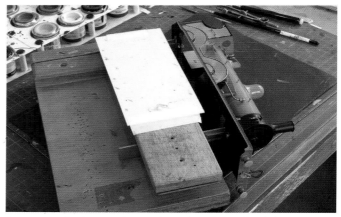

Left: The assembly is then fixed to the base with a single wood screw. The slotted hole gives me more freedom to make use of any existing hole in the ply. As you can see, I have many holes to choose from. The actual location of the fixing is found by sliding the platform up to the underside of both buffer and drag beams. When it is in contact with both, the bracket can be screwed down. Right: The platform is placed on top, using the most convenient of the three guides. It is pushed up to the underside of the buffer and drag beams, and then the Plastikard is positioned so that it is a tight fit against the underside of the footplate and hard against the back of the buffer beam or drag beam. It is then fixed down with tape.

In use, the Plastikard is now firmly located so that the centre point of the circle remains in the same place even if the platform is removed and replaced. To line out the other side of the engine, the wood screw is released, the 8BA screw loosened and the fixing bracket rotated through 180°. The whole lot is then flipped over and re-fixed the other way up. The Plastikard will need repositioning and new centres found – if the dividers are still set for the correct radius it will be so much quicker to do.

DRAWING A CURVE WITH COMPASSES

Luckily, I have a pair of spring bow pen compasses which I bought as part of a set when a student. They are British made by Thornton, sadly no longer with us, and are extremely good. However, Haff spring bow compasses are still available (see suppliers list). This method is useful for lining splashers where there is no edge to follow (see below), and making transfers for inaccessible areas. The first problem is finding the centre of the arc and, having found it, the second is having somewhere to stick the compass point.

The centre of a splasher arc will not be the wheel centre but it should, of course, be somewhere near but, as you should not have the chassis fixed in while painting, it is academic.

One method of fixing the centre point is to build a frame to hold the model, as I have done (see photos), or cut a piece of thick plastic card and slide it into position under the valance, hard against the underside of footplate and either buffer beam or drag beam. This will locate it positively so that it can be replaced in exactly the same position for any second arc.

I find the centre of the circle by trial and error, using dividers. As I do quite a lot of it, I can do it quite quickly. Set the dividers to the approximate radius and put one point on the top centre of the splasher edge and the other as close to the centre line as you can guess. Make a light mark in the plastic card. Swing the dividers and check if the pivot point is on the centre line and whether the radius needs to increase or decrease. Move the point accordingly, adjust the radius and try again. Repeat until the point of the dividers follows the edge of the splasher exactly. Make a decent indentation for the compasses point and mark it with a pencil. Now that the radius is fixed, you must not alter the dividers' setting until you have found the centre point for each of the other splashers.

Having found the centre, you can draw the arc with the compasses and hopefully next day replace the card in exactly the same position and draw in an adjacent colour.

You will need to use this method for finding the centre of any arc traced off the model if you wish to make a transfer by using centre compasses.

One problem that I have found, particularly with 00 gauge models that have sandboxes integral with splashers, is that, because the splasher is slightly larger than scale, to cope with the overscale flanges, the lining does not come out like that in the photograph. This is because the lining on the sand box is pushed out of position by the large splasher. For this case a little deception or *trompe l'oeil* is required. Reduce the splasher lining radius slightly and move the centre of the curve back a little so that the sand box lining takes on more correct proportions.

The holding frame in 4mm mode without the distance piece attached.

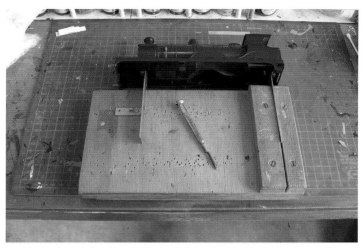

With the platform and Plastikard in place, dividers are used to find the centre of the curve. I place the point where I think the centre may be, and then swing the dividers to check if I am right. If not, I adjust the radius and centre point and repeat until I find the centre point. There is no alternative to trial and error for this stage. Having found the first centre, I mark the point with a pencil circle. I have to do this because there are already dozens of holes in the Plastikard. Without changing the setting of the dividers, I find the centre of the other splasher and mark that.

The loco body is fitted into the frame for lining the cab side. As the rear splasher forms part of the cab side, there is no edge for using as an offset for the compasses. As a last resort, the beading itself could be used for the offset but it is easier to draw the curve from a centre point.

I then put in all the lining from the two marked centres using the spring bow compasses.

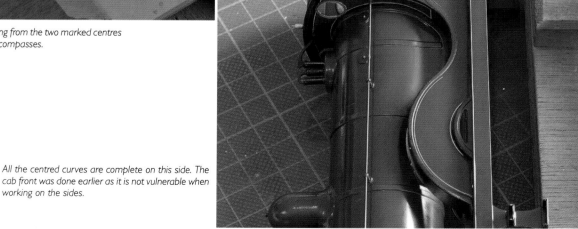

All the centred curves are complete on this side. The cab front was done earlier as it is not vulnerable when working on the sides.

FOLLOWING AN EDGE WITH COMPASSES (OFFSETTING)

I use this method where I can as it is particularly useful in producing a precise line where there is a compound curve. I replace the point in the compasses with a short length of 1mm brass wire, rounded at the end – which is less harsh on paintwork. This is called the guide wire. The compasses are then set to the edge distance and then, with the guide wire running along the edge, a line is drawn at a precise distance from the edge and, equally precisely, a similar shape to the edge. The method is very good for valances, splashers, step plates, tender frames and top edges of tenders. The system, however, falls down completely if the edges are not true. The usual culprit is etching tabs not filed flat. The other problems are with applied beading not bedded down properly and not following the correct curve, or splasher tops not following the same arc as the sides.

The method has to be practised. As the compasses follow the curve, they must be kept normal to the edge. If they are not, the distance of the line from the edge will reduce and the width of the line may vary.

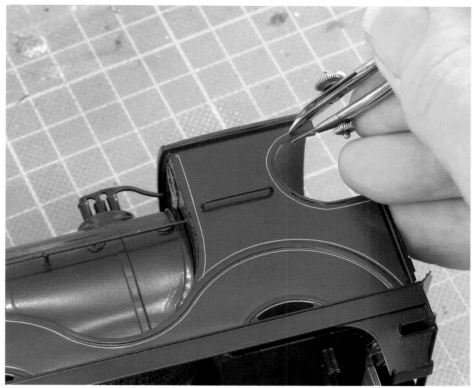

The two splasher curves are joined using offset compasses and further lining is drawn onto the cab side.

Offsetting work continues with the foot-step backing plates and the drop at the front of the valance. Finally, the remaining straight lines are filled in with the bow pen, finishing with the vulnerable valance edge. After a day's drying time, the black line is drawn adjacent to the white, using the same methods in the same sequence. The black edging can then be filled in with a brush. When that is dry, the body is released from the wood block, turned over and refixed to do the other side. Meanwhile both sides and back of the tender are lined.

The outer lines on the cab front were done by offsetting from the edge. The boiler bands are transfers, as is the top part of the cab angle. The cab front inner line and the lower part of the cab angle are brushwork. If you were building the kit you would use a boiler spacer to establish the radius of the cab front inner line and make a transfer for that awkward bit of lining.

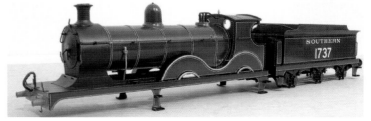

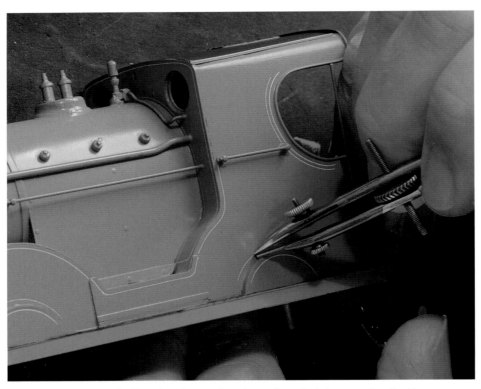

GNRI No. 171. The awkward curves above the coupling rod splashers were done like this.

When using this method for the curves and a normal pen for the straights, the curves must be drawn first, and then joined together by the straight lines. It cannot be done the other way around.

If the straight edges of the model are true and there are no obstructions 'around the corner', this method can also be used to draw the straight lines on the model. It is particularly useful on buffer planks. Straight lines on a curved part of the model (around buffer stocks, cylinder covers, splasher tops, etc) can readily be done by this method.

If using this method to do all the lines on the valance, especially double lining in the LMS 1946 style and BR Standard Pacifics, all lines must be drawn from the same edge.

If you are restoring a vintage model that has hand-painted boiler band lining, the compasses can be used to follow the edge of the boiler band. It's not easy but sometimes it is the only way. For this method to work, the paint has to be quite thick to reduce blobbing, as the pen will be stopping and starting quite often.

This photograph shows the extent of lining that can be done without using a ruler.

It is possible to use quite large offsets to get to awkward situations. If you are lining a buffer plank, it would be normal to offset from the adjacent edge but the top edge is often obstructed by lamp brackets, so this can be lined by running the guide along the bottom edge. I have used offsets of up to 2in (50mm) to reach lines otherwise obstructed.

DRAWING CURVES BY 'DOTTING IN'

Just occasionally, none of the above methods may work so the last resort is drawing a curve as a series of contiguous dots, using a rest to steady the pen. The rest may be a straight edge or curved template or even part of the model itself.

When using this technique, the paint in the pen needs to be fairly thick, so that it does not flood out each time the pen makes contact. It's a slow job and you may need a few goes before you get an acceptable line. With a bit of brushwork and error correction, you will get there in the end.

It's not a method I use much as my brushing skills have improved over the years, but it is useful for the front end of the streamlined Coronations.

A difficult curve to put in is the one above a coupling rod splasher. This feature was common on pre-grouping engines and, of course, lasted into BR days. See the M7 on page 57.

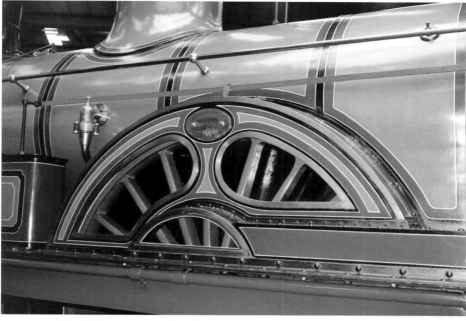

Preserved NER 901 Class locomotive. I haven't been asked to paint one of these yet. At first glance the lining on the splasher looks to be a nightmare but, on further examination, I can see that each line, apart from around the works plate, is parallel to an edge so, in theory, given a well constructed model, each line can be drawn by using offset compasses.

Lining a buffer beam. This Great Central tender has a white line along the sides and bottom edge only, with a black border. Needless to say, the edges must be filed smooth before painting. There will be gaps at obstructions that will need filling with a fine brush. The white line goes on first, after checking that the red paint has covered well and is smooth enough (if it has been brushed on).

Lining a Great Central number plate. This is a Guilplates 7mm scale number plate, which has to be filed accurately to shape as the compasses follow the edge to place the line in the correct position.

MIXED TRAFFIC LINING

This 0 gauge Ivatt 2P was a lining-only job. Here the cream line is visible and it certainly looks better than simple red/grey lining. On the internal corners it is the red line that has the 4in radius and the cream and grey reduced to suit.

Nigel Smith's ex GW Saint in 7mm, built from the Slater's kit. I think it looks smart in BR lined black but the purists would probably disagree. The lining is fairly simple on this engine as the Western Region abandoned lining on the hanging bar (valance) after the first few repaints. The main lining difficulty on the engine is the complex curve that follows the cab cut-out. This was done using the compasses offset from the edge; all the other curves were done with a fine brush. I do the cream line first and then, on day 2, the grey and red. Following objections that the red number plates were less legible, the WR reverted to black plates (lined in red, for lined black locomotives).

The curves on the splasher and name plate were all executed with compasses following the edge. The Western Region went its own way as far as splasher lining was concerned. The official specification was that only the top curve should be lined in grey and cream, but the WR continued to line the bottom edge, as the GWR had done.

ORDER OF LINING

It is important to work out the order in which the lining is executed so as to achieve the best quality of line, the most accurate position of line and, very importantly, the least damage to existing lines. Unfortunately, there are some conflicting requirements.

1) *The most delicate lines of the lightest colour should be done first.*

The light colours are the ones you see first, they are the ones that stand out and are therefore considerably more critical than the remainder. The essence of lining is to do the light, delicate lines first and work on them until they are absolutely spot on before moving on to the darker colours.

Also, for drawing the most delicate lines, the pen needs a virgin surface. The pen is a sensitive instrument and if you are drawing a line immediately adjacent to another one, which may have imperfections

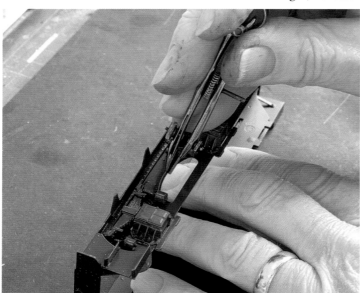 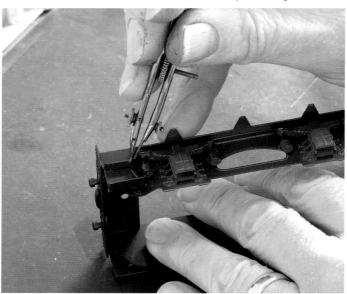

Left: *Using the compasses to offset a line from the edge makes lining the tender frames relatively simple. This is the gold line (P984 Brass) going on.* Right: *The step plates are also done with the compasses. Where the pen blades touched the underside of the step, a bit of gold was deposited. This happens all the time when squeezing into tight spots, so the odd bits of paint have to be removed or painted over.*

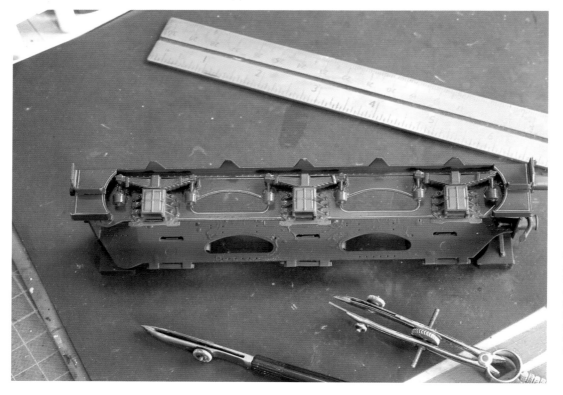

The frames almost complete. There is an awkward bit to do at the front end up to the brake rod bearing and at the rear behind the footsteps. These parts are always fiddly; if you can get a pen in, fine, if not then it's a transfer or fine brushwork. Even the rear boiler band can be put in if the adjacent edge is good – and the boiler is a separate part.

along its edge, the pen may jump over them or be knocked off course. It follows therefore, that if the most delicate line is the first one down, you are working in the lowest risk situation.

2) *Where a line consists of both straight and curved portions (drawn by offsetting with compasses), the curved part should be done first.*
Because the compasses put the line at a fixed distance from the edge, it is easier to join the straight portion to the curve than vice versa.

3) *Where the lining consists of a group of lines, the line nearest the edge should be first.*
Because the setting out of the lining is always done by measuring in from the edge it is more accurate to do the line nearest the edge first and then work inwards.

4) *The least vulnerable lines should be first.*
At the risk of sounding like the Health and Safety Commission, this is where you need to do a risk assessment to ascertain which lines are the most vulnerable to being messed up simply by handling the model.

Wet lining paint is always susceptible to damage from fingers, resting a ruler on it or contact with the surface the model is resting on. Valance lining, in particular, is vulnerable to finger damage and so should be the last to go on. Projections from the body, such as beading, hand rails and steps, will prevent the ruler from touching the wet lining, so lines thus protected are less vulnerable. Lining on a transverse surface, such as the front of the cab or back of tender, is less likely to be handled than the body sides, so they should be lined early in the sequence.

You will need to assess where your hand or finger is going to rest when using the pen so that you don't snooker yourself; can you, for example, safely lay a ruler down without smudging existing wet lining. If you have plenty of time to complete the lining, it is best to do a bit, let it dry, then do a bit more. If you are pushed for time, it will pay you to do a dry run and work out the most efficient way to tackle the lining. If you don't, I can guarantee that you will smudge wet lining and waste time correcting it.

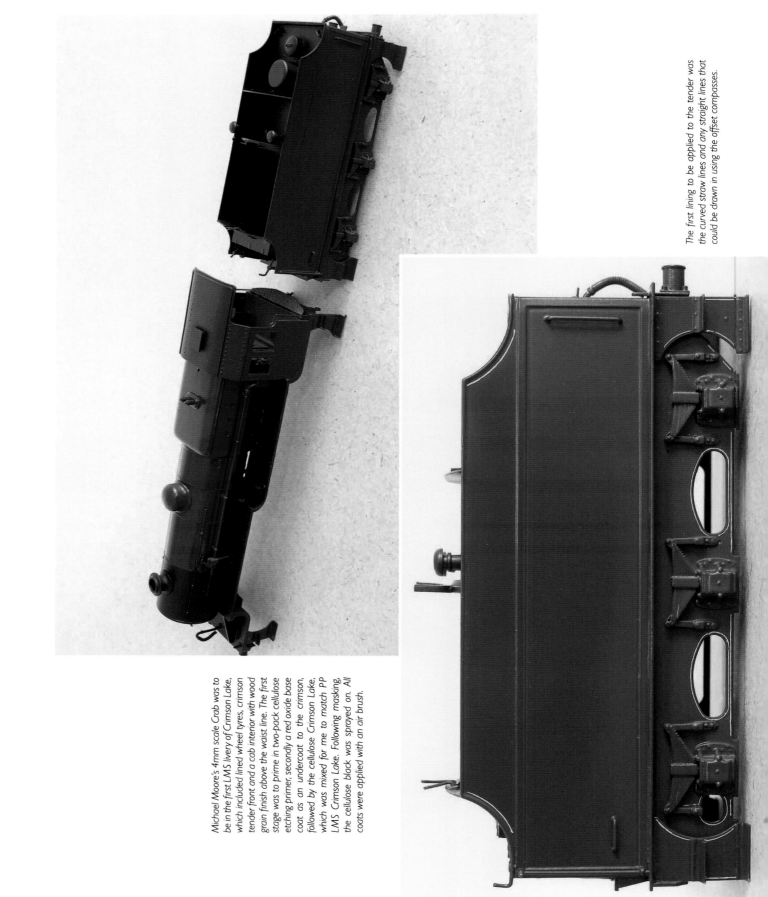

Michael Moore's 4mm scale Crab was to be in the first LMS livery of Crimson Lake, which included lined wheel tyres, crimson tender front and a cab interior with wood grain finish above the waist line. The first stage was to prime in two-pack cellulose etching primer, secondly a red oxide base coat as an undercoat to the crimson, followed by the cellulose Crimson Lake, which was mixed for me to match PP LMS Crimson Lake. Following masking, the cellulose black was sprayed on. All coats were applied with an air brush.

The first lining to be applied to the tender was the curved straw lines and any straight lines that could be drawn in using the offset compasses.

LMS CRIMSON LAKE ENGINES 1923–1936, WITH 'STRAW' LINING

This was followed by the remaining straight lines using pen and straight edge. You can see that some of the lines are incomplete at the ends where the pen was obstructed by projections.

The straw lining completed with the fine brush and tidied up by lifting unwanted paint. Unfortunately, the tie bars on this model are too slender, leaving little room for the lining. On the prototype there is a much wider band of crimson between the straw lines.

Using the same principles as above, a black line was drawn against each straw line and then the edges were filled in with H Gloss Black, using a brush. Note that I am using a rest to give my hand stability and to avoid touching the fresh paintwork.

The tender side complete except for the axle boxes and springs. These were brush painted, with a second division brush. Provided you work out a system for painting these awkward areas you can conserve brushes and sanity. How much easier if they had been left off for separate spraying – and the lining would have been simpler too. The tender buffer plank and buffer housings have been painted in H Primer Grey as an undercoat for the red. The vacuum hose can be left in base coat until after varnishing as it will receive a matt black or dark grey.

The tender rear nearly complete. No ruler or transfers were used for the lining; it was all done from the edge with compasses. The top straw line seems to be low but this is how they were – it has to line up with the sides. Note that LMS buffer housing rims were black, with a straw line separating them from the red. Yet another case of lining from the edge with compasses. A transfer is possible instead, but it would have to be well soaked in decal softener to get it to sit around such a tight curve. I'm not too sure about the red plates, but that is how they came.

The tender front. Details of liveries in this sort of area are like hens' teeth. I have a photograph of this type of tender front dated 1930 that shows lining along the top of the tool box and around the coal hole but none around the top of the coal plate. This would indicate that the tender front was crimson and the coal plate black. This is the way that the preserved Midland Compound tender is painted. However, there is also a photograph of a Crab in Locomotives of the LMS, Volume 5 (Jenkinson & Essery, etc) that shows, just, lining on the coal plate. Rightly or wrongly, I opted to paint the lot in crimson with the lining as shown. It would have been quite easy had the brake and scoop pillars not been there. In the event I used compasses where I could and brushed in the remainder.

By comparison with the tender, the lining on the engine was straightforward. The cab side straights were done with pen and ruler while the valance and steps were done with compasses. The only brushwork was on the two curves on the cab sides. Where the hand rails are a different colour from the body, insert a trapezoidal piece of card behind to protect the body paint. As an alternative, a cute way to paint the rails is with a bow pen – open the points up until the gap is about half the diameter of the rail, then it should guide itself along, with care.

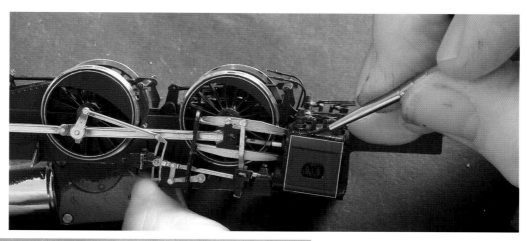

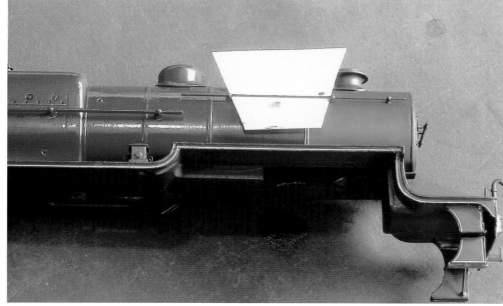

The cylinders received the same paint treatment as the superstructure. All the lining was ruled on, then the outer black areas filled in by brush. The wheels were edge lined with compasses while still on the chassis.

The completed locomotive. The cab interior was brush painted, black below the waist and H Matt Sand above. The latter was then overpainted, to create an oak grain effect, with PP M&GN Engine Brown, let down with a little linseed oil. The transfers are HMRS Methfix. It was all finished with Ronseal Polyurethane Gloss varnish with a little PP Matting agent to give it a pleasing finish just on the gloss side of satin. It just needs glazing and coaling up (and possibly a little weathering?).

LMS CRIMSON LAKE ENGINES 1937-1939, WITH YELLOW LINING

The LMS Princess Class certainly had a presence; it was the Pacific that the Great Western never had. This 0 gauge model was built by Graham Varley from the David Andrews kit. LMS Crimson Lake needs a red-brown under-coat to give it depth and help coverage. If using aerosols, a red oxide primer will suit but in this case I used a cellulose red oxide 'base coat', which has no added filler and dries to a smooth satin sheen. The top coat is a cellulose paint I had matched to PP Crimson Lake. The lining on LMS engines is quite straightforward (for me) as a great deal of it can be done with compasses fol-lowing the edge. The bottom line at the back of the tender passes over the body fixing brackets so, in this case, I opted to make and use a transfer. Seven pieces in all and a b ..... to line up!

SOME PRE-GROUPING LIVERIES

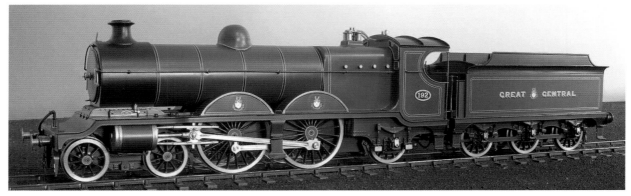

The 'Jersey Lily' of the Great Central Railway. This is a Gladiator 7mm scale kit that I built. One of David Andrews's designs, it builds straight out of the box; the only modification I made was to make the rear axle a pony instead of sliding in the frames. Having built it, I was able to make sure that all the edges were flat and smooth so that the compasses glided along the edges when doing the lining. My principal error was to fix the boiler permanently to the running plate, which made lining the top and back of the splashers difficult. The circles on the splasher faces, around the coats of arms, were done by drilling a tiny indentation in the centre of the circle and using this to locate the compasses' point. The centre point was then hidden by the coat of arms transfer (Guilplates). The wheels are by Alan Harris, which were a pleasure to line, being cast iron complete with centre pops on the axle ends. The engine picks up the electricity on ten wheels by the 'Improved American' method. The AGH wheels came insulated on one side only (this is an option) so that all the wheels on the engine pick up from one side. The tender chassis is insulated from the body to allow double heading. The tender wheels pick up from the other side plus two wipers on the back of the insulated drivers. This means that the loco chassis can be tested on its own, without the tender. An RG7 motor and a boiler full of lead give it plenty of power and adhesion.

Loch Maree *is a 00 gauge DJH whitemetal kit built by Mike Edge. The Jones II livery ranks alongside the Wainwright SECR style in terms of difficulty but is less well documented. I got the basic details from* Highland Railway Liveries *by H. Geddes and E. Bellass, but there were still some areas that were unclear.*

A 00 gauge T9 in Drummond livery. The importance of getting the curves of the top of the splashers correct is particularly relevant in the case of the T9. The most dominant line is that from the top of the cab side down to the front of the splashers; a continuous sweep of the compasses does it, but if the pen is thrown out of line by badly seated splasher tops it will mean lots of remedial work.

This 0 gauge 'Claud Hamilton', was scratchbuilt by Mike Edge using his own etchings for the splashers, cab and elaborate valances. Despite the apparent complexity of the lining, if the edges are true, the compasses will take the pen where it needs to go. The cab roof, being white, has merged into the background. The GER was very pragmatic, it painted the front of the cab in plain black; no painting problems there then. The transfers are by Guilplates.

GWR/BR GREEN LOCOMOTIVE LINING

This 7mm scale model of a GWR Saint has been scratch built but, unfortunately, I don't know the name of the builder. The lining on Great Western boiler bands tended to be more complex than on other railways. The lining on the firebox, for example, was not continued over the top but stopped at the point where it became horizontal and the two orange lines closed off by joining them together. The black line stopped about half an inch short of that. At the base of the firebox, the lines ended in a semi-circular curve around a rivet head (these are better illustrated on the City of Truro photographs). Similarly, the lining on the front boiler band was closed off adjacent to the cover on the right-hand side, just above the ejector pipe. On some classes, the feed pipe covers were lined, as shown here. Given a pair of offset compasses and a steady hand, it is not as daunting as it might appear. The lining on the weatherboard follows all the edges and so becomes quite complex. The angle-iron joining the weatherboard to the roof and cab side sheets was, however, painted green. On later engines, this angle was within the cab, so those engines were lined differently. The angle-iron joining the weatherboard and firebox cladding was lined as a half boiler band, and that lining was continued on the cladding over the top of the rear splasher. It makes it so much easier if the firebox and cab are separate units, then at least you get a fighting chance of getting a pen near the lining. The ejector pipe and reverser rod are black, inevitably brush painted after the spraying is finished.

Ex-GWR No. 4174 is a 7mm scale model built by Nigel Smith from the Martin Finney kit. No. 4160 was photographed on the West Somerset Railway.

This is the Adams T3 Class from the 0 gauge Finney kit. Rather an elegant locomotive as many of his designs were. Part of the lining process has been illustrated elsewhere. The bogie wheel splashers were lined, as usual from the edge, but in this case the lower edge was a little uneven, so both were drawn in using the top edge as a guide, which at least made them parallel. The ends were joined with a brush.

As a change from blue engines, this is the Caledonian goods livery. I reversed my normal rule here and did the red line first, not the brighter white line. The red went through the tank side bolts and therefore its position was rather more critical than the white.

LINING WHEELS

There are various styles of lining for wheels, some of which are simple to do, but others are b-----s. The most simple is the rim line that separates the rim from the tyre. The simplest way of doing that is by offsetting from the tread. This would be followed by a touching line in the tyre colour, so that the tyre can then be brush painted up to this line.

Lining at the centre of the wheel presents more problems and may warrant a bit of preparation at the planning stage. There are two types of lining at the centre, which I will call wheel boss lining and axle end lining.

The wheel boss lining follows the edge of the boss adjacent to the spokes and so, for a driving wheel, it is not a complete circle as it also goes around the crankpin boss. This type of line is also best drawn by offsetting. There should be just enough of a lip for the guide to follow. If the base of the spokes intrudes into this space, the best you can do is set out a series of dots and then join them up by brush.

Axle end lining is not really on the end of the axle but on the boss adjacent to the axle hole. The easiest way to do this is from the centre of the axle using normal compasses. If you enjoy the luxury of AGH wheels that come ready centre-popped, it's a comparative doddle. I have a centre-drilled 6BA screw for lining Slater's wheels and a centre-drilled Romford axle for Romford/Markits wheels. The problems occur when faced with lining push-on wheels such as Ultrascale, Sharman and Gibson where the axle ends are never centre-popped. If you are building the engine and propose using these wheels, it is a good idea to centre pop them yourself before assembly, or get a friend with a lathe to do it. Failing that, it's careful brushwork together with doing as much as possible by offsetting from the boss edge. The Great Western, in its wisdom, had double circles round its axle ends during the Indian Red wheels period!

The axle ends of push-on wheels can be lined before the wheels go on by offsetting from the axle hole. This does carry the risk of damage while pushing the wheels on.

The cranks on outside-frame locomotives were often lined, both around the edge and around the axle end. The former can easily be done by offsetting and the latter from the axle centre, or offsetting half and brushing half.

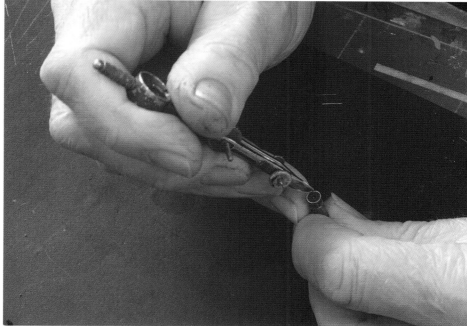

Another solution to both the push-on wheel and outside crank, as there is no wheel nut to worry about, is to make a transfer.

It pays to dress plastic outside cranks before fixing as the edges can be a bit ragged.

Even Slater's wheel screws have to be lined sometimes. These are for the bogie wheel centres.

Following the application of etching primer, in this case Phoenix Precision Two Part, the Indian Red areas were sprayed with P6 Gloss GWR Indian Red 1881 – 1906. This strange colour appears to change its hue in each photograph, even in photographs of the prototype. Beware of using photos to check colour! The Indian Red was sprayed on first because it is easier to mask it from the green, rather than the other way around. As the dark green has good cover, there was no need to mask off any other areas.

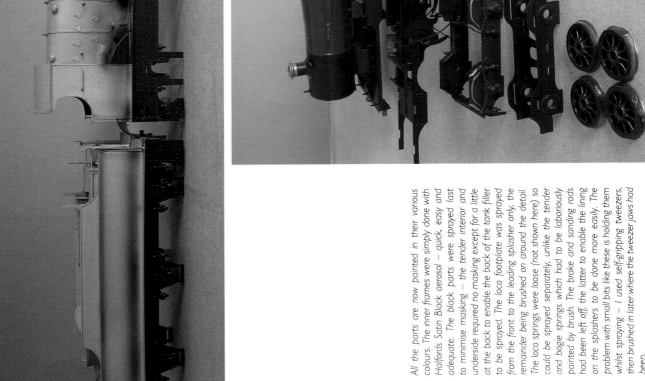

All the parts are now painted in their various colours. The inner frames were simply done with Halfords Satin Black aerosol – quick, easy and adequate. The black parts were sprayed last to minimise masking – the tender interior and underside required no masking except for a little at the back to enable the back of the tank filler to be sprayed. The loco footplate was sprayed from the front to the leading splasher only, the remainder being brushed on around the detail. The loco springs were loose (not shown here) so could be sprayed separately, unlike the tender and bogie springs which had to be laboriously painted by brush. The brake and sanding rods had been left off, the latter to enable the lining on the splashers to be done more easily. The problem with small bits like these is holding them whilst spraying – I used self-gripping tweezers, then brushed in later where the tweezer jaws had been.

GREAT WESTERN RAILWAY – DOUBLE LINING STYLE

When I was planning the book, I thought it would be a good idea to show in detail the painting of an engine from each of the Big Four. Unfortunately, when it came to the Great Western, all I had available within the allotted time span was the *City of Truro*. An obviously ambitious project but, nevertheless, all the principles are the same as those for a more simple scheme. *City of Truro*, as far as I am aware, never received the double lining style when in service but was given it when it was returned to steam between 1957 – 1961. It was in plain green as No. 3717 in the Great Western Museum from then until 1985, when it was again returned to steam and regained its elaborate livery. The model carries the present version of that livery, which differs from the more authentic one carried previously.

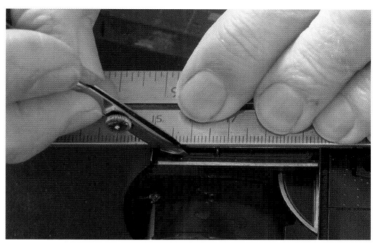

Cab fronts are always the most difficult to line as access is so limited and the shapes awkward. Here the vertical lines adjacent to the beading on the lower part were executed with the compasses, but all the rest were brushed on. The lining above the firebox is a mix of offset compass work (the top curve) and brush for the remainder. Logically, this should be double lining as it is lower down, but this is as the engine is presently painted – and I am not complaining.

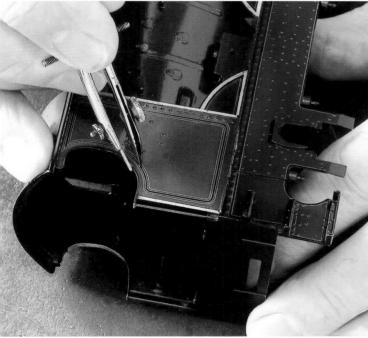

The four orange lines following the curve of the cab cut-out were done with offset compasses but the black line can be done either with compasses or with a brush.

The completed cab side. The paint was scraped off the brass beading after each painting stage. Unfortunately, the cut-out beading was not as true a curve as it could have been, so the lining had to be tweaked a little to create a better curve.

The boiler bands were drawn onto green-painted blank transfer (waterslide) paper. Because there were five lines of colour in each boiler band, I drew out three times as many as I needed. Two strips have already been lifted.

The semi-circular ends of the rear three boiler bands are drawn in with the fine brush beyond the edge of the transfer.

A close-up of the splasher and crank. With the spring and sand box rod in place, the splasher lining would have been a much more difficult proposition. The curve was drawn from the edge and the straight from a short length of brass angle ledged on the edge of the footplate to clear the rivets thereon. I attempted to line the crank from the edge but, unfortunately, it was not a sufficiently true circle, so the bad bits were lifted and the rest filled in with a brush. Also visible in this view is the top feed pipe cover, which is lined similarly to a boiler band but, being curved, will not take a transfer. The solution was again to use the compasses. Opening them to a little over a millimetre enabled them to sit over the curve of the cover and give enough stability to draw a line around the curve of the pipe cover. Five lines in fact. The sand boxes on the prototype City of Truro, as presently painted, are green but they should be Indian Red.

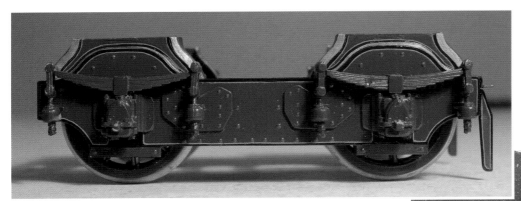

The bogie side, before painting the springs black. The lining is again compasses and brush work.

The wheels were re-inserted in the chassis before the brake hangers were lined. This was to give some protection to them during the lining process; it was somewhere to rest the fingers and it protected the hangers on the other side from touching the work top when their paint was wet. The lining was ruled on, with the end curves brushed in.

The initial phase of lining the tender. The various setting-out marks can be seen dotted about the edges. The bottom angle of the tender was not quite straight on this model; if you look closely, it rises a little towards the centre, so the datum had to be two paint dots at front and rear, set out from the bottom corners. From these all the other setting-out points were measured with dividers or marked with compasses. Drawing so many parallel lines is not easy and some of those pictured were lifted and redrawn as they were not satisfactory.

All the corners were brushed in, 128 of them
(seven panels of 16 plus the coal plates).

Nearly there. It looks a bit messy at this stage but, providing a gloss paint has been used, any smudges can be wiped away with a dry cloth later.

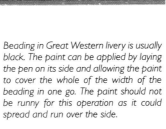

Beading in Great Western livery is usually black. The paint can be applied by laying the pen on its side and allowing the paint to cover the whole of the width of the beading in one go. The paint should not be runny for this operation as it could spread and run over the side.

The completed tender, HMRS Methfix transfer applied and the whole given a coat of satin varnish. The tool boxes on a GWR tender were green – ideally not fixed until after painting (see PLANNING). These were painted along with the sides and then masked off while the tender inner was sprayed black. The lining on the horn guides is scarfed at the bottom.

This 7mm scale contractor's engine's livery was copied from a photograph, more or less. I was given a free hand on its interpretation, so I lined the inside of the cab as well. The cab roof is removable so all the interesting curly bits could be done with offset compasses from the adjacent edge. Photo by BARRY NORMAN

Working, from a reasonable photograph, the size and spacing of the letters are calculated.

The actual spacing of the letters is marked onto a strip of paper, which is then attached to the model with masking tape. The height of the letters above the footplate is marked at each end of the tanks by using the compasses. Using the marks on tanks and paper, the outlines of the letters are drawn. The horizontals are drawn with a ruler lined up with the height marks at the edge and the verticals are drawn using a small set-square. The limits of the curved letters are marked with a dot or short dash.

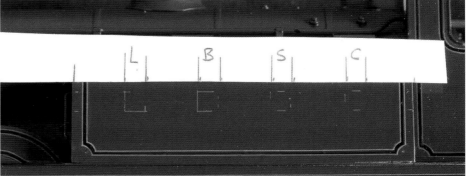

Using another photograph (of a different class of locomotive, in this case), which is more broadside on, the lettering is copied.

CHAPTER SIX

HAND LETTERING AND NUMBERING

This is one of the most daunting tasks for the inexperienced, but, provided your approach and execution is methodical, it may not be as bad as you thought.

This time the alliterative key is Size, Shape and Spacing. Hopefully, your reference work will tell you what the height of the lettering is and from that you can measure or estimate the different widths of letter. If you do not have a written specification for the lettering size, you will need to scale off from the photograph you are using for the setting out.

For those who have forgotten the maths, or never learnt it in the first place, this is the method to use. Unless you have the perfect broadside photo, you will have to be aware of the effects of perspective, both horizontally and vertically, although the latter's effect is very small. In the example of the LBSC E5X tank, I measured the height of the model's side tank and the height of the side tank in the photograph. Because of perspective, I measured the height of the tank in the photo through the centre line of the nearest letter. I also measured the height of that letter. All the measurements were taken with dividers as this is more accurate than using a ruler direct.

The scale = height of model tank ÷ height of photo tank
The height of the model letter = height of photo letter x scale

If you get muddled up during the calculations, just remember that if the model is larger than the photo, the lettering will be larger, and vice versa.

The spacing is more problematical. If you have the broadside photograph it is a simple matter of direct measurement and scaling. If you only have a three-quarter front view of your particular engine, then you may need to look at photos of other engines of that company to ascertain the theory behind the setting out and then translate that to yours.

If you haven't even got that, then you will have to estimate. For company initials, the spaces between the letters will be equal but the end spaces may be different. The LBSC had equal spaces from the edges of the tanks and between each letter, ignoring the lining. Other companies had half spaces from the lining to the letter and full spaces between the letters, or full spaces from

lining to letter. Inspection of your photo should show what was going on.

What I do then is write down the measurements of the spaces and letter widths, add them up and check that they equal the space available, and adjust as necessary. I then cut out a strip of paper and measure out on it the model dimensions of all the spaces and letters. I then stick the strip to the model above or below the line of lettering.

The next thing to do is to find where the lettering was positioned in relation to the height of the side. Usually the lettering was centred just above the centre line of the side or lining panel. This was done by measurement or by including the blocking or shading in the total height of the letter so that the centre of the letter proper ended up just above the centre of the panel. If the lettering on your model is not somewhere near the centre line you will need to scale off from the photo.

With compasses, using the footplate as a datum, I put a dot at each end of the tank

at the level of the bottom of the letters and repeat for the top level. I then rule in the straight bits of the top and bottom of each letter using the paper strip as a guide to horizontal position. If the letters are rounded, I put a dot. With a setsquare I rule in the verticals using the guide lines on the paper strip; again rounded letters are dotted.

Next I lift any unwanted paint. I then put in the outlines of the curved letters with a fine brush and rule in the sloping bit of A's and W's (difficult). I then turn the whole thing around so that I am looking at the letters upside-down. This is where errors in letter shapes can be seen. From here on it is 'fill in and fudge'. Fill in the outlines, add in the middle strokes of B, E, F, P and R, lift unwanted paint, all with continual reference to the photograph to achieve a good letter shape.

To help with the slope of A's and W's, measure the angle of slope on the photo and then make a small plastic card set square with the hypotenuse at the same slope. Use

The letters are finished with shading and then the number is started, following similar principles.

Below: *The numbers are filled in and await some shading, which is not added until the ochre paint is dry.*

it to draw in one side of the letter and then flip it over to do the other side. This should produce a perfectly equal letter.

Once it is dry, the blocking and/or shading can be added, which is a much simpler job, but this is when the letters come to life and you can start to enjoy the result of your efforts. This stage can be used to correct the letter shapes by over painting, but it should not be relied upon; try to get it right first time. Blocking can be quite complex, with numerous colours and shades – and different colours for different backgrounds. For example, on green

The numbers were more of a fiddle as they are mostly rounded shapes. They were set out with a series of dots and dashes and then outlines drawn in, with constant reference to a photograph to achieve the best shape.

LNER engines the blocking is red and black, with white highlights; on black engines it is red and brown, ditto; and on buffer planks it is brown and black, ditto.

The painting of complete words, rather than company initials, is rather more fraught. For a start, there are more letters to do and they are smaller, but the spacing, which is an art not a science, is the most important part. If you have not done any formal lettering before, it is worthwhile actually studying how letters and spacing work together. Copy your letters out in pencil to a larger scale on paper then stand back and see if it looks right. Any errors in the spacing should become evident.

Sometimes the spacing is different in different words. In both BRITISH RAIL-WAYS and GREAT WESTERN applied to locomotives, the shorter word had more widely spaced letters to give it more weight.

If your natural handwriting slopes, then you must make doubly sure the model lettering doesn't slope in the same way – I've seen that so many times on models. Use a setsquare.

The result. Other points to note are that the white lining on the lower edge of the cab passes through the line of rivets. This is best achieved with pretty thick paint, as thin paint will form a blob each time it passes over a rivet. Any thickenings that do occur will need to be removed in the usual manner. The window frames in LNER days were varnished wood. The edges can be ruled in and then filled by brush. There is lining inside the cab (just visible), which is best achieved by using compasses, with the edge as the template. Likewise the red footplate valance lining, but only if the underside of the valance is smooth and true.

A general view of the nearly complete engine. She just needs name and works plates (and a bit of judicious weathering?). Whether or not you like Thompson Pacifics, I think it is an impressive model.

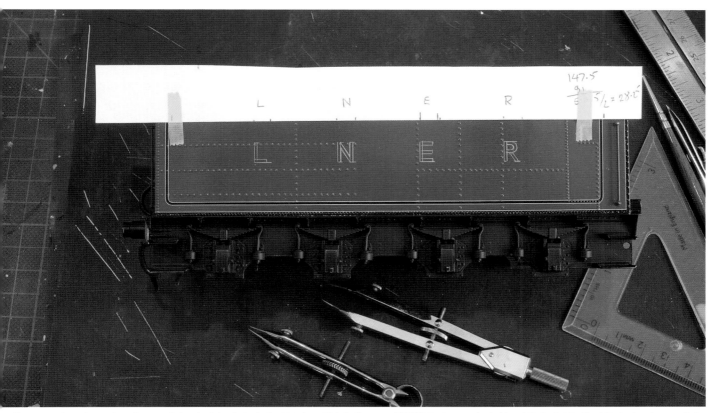

The next task on the tender, after completing the lining, is to do the lettering, which, in the case of LNER postwar unshaded, is relatively simple. The lettering has been scaled from a photograph, the letter size and spacing calculated (both between the letters and between the lining, top, bottom and sides). I generally draw out the spacing on a strip of paper, which I then stick to the model. I draw in the vertical lines with pen and setsquare and dot in the limits of the curved letters. I then rule in the horizontals from measured setting-out points and then the remaining straight lines that run at an angle and finally brush in the curves. The lettering is then filled in by brush and the unwanted bits of paint removed in the usual way. You can see from the pencil marks adjacent to the lining that the lettering has been moved slightly back to avoid the line of rivets interfering with the 'E' and 'R'.

A general view of the cab side and leading edge of the tender. LNER green locomotives had green, lined engine wheels but plain black tender wheels.

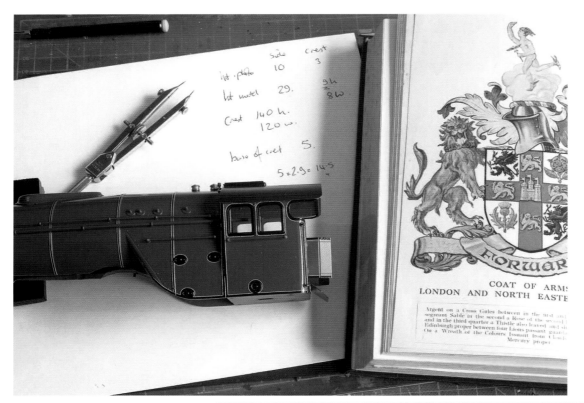

When first preserved, Flying Scotsman had the LNER coat-of-arms on the cab sides. I needed to scale the coat-of-arms from a photograph, which is what the calculations are for. The coat-of-arms to be copied is in the book to the right of the photograph. Just visible on the model are the setting-out dots.

The completed coat-of-arms on the cab side. It is only 9mm high by 8mm wide.

One of Whitelegge's lumps of metal. A 7mm scale model scratchbuilt by Mike Edge. On the prototype engines the boiler cladding was not painted but left as blued steel. I represented that by adding some blue paint to black and spraying some trial pieces and matching to some blued steel. There are some G&SWR transfers available from the G&SWR Society but, unfortunately, not in the larger size used on this engine, so the lettering is painted on. I commissioned Diane Carney to do the works plates for the bunker sides but they had not yet arrived when the photograph was taken. Again the crimson areas were painted first to ease masking.

This is a typical 'works grey' photograph, useful in showing the location of the lining but less so in showing colour boundaries. I checked this photo against working condition locomotives to make sure the lining had not been made over-elaborate for publicity purposes.

This 7mm scale model of Caledonian Railway Cardean was scratchbuilt by Mike Edge. The highlighted silver and brass work were added by his customer. A great deal of the complex lining was done by using offset compasses following the adjacent edge. The coats-of-arms and lettering are Fox transfers but the name and front number were done by hand. The name presented a number of difficulties as each letter is at a different angle. The top and bottom limits for the name were marked out as a series of dots with compasses, after finding the centre of the curve. The lettering was started at the 'D' and roughed in, with a very 'light touch' paint, a letter at a time, to the 'C' and 'N'. The spacing was adjusted by lifting unwanted portions of letters and filling out others. At this setting-out stage, the letters are very lightly painted to avoid having to move too much paint around, and create smears. The angle of each letter also has to be checked by comparing it to the edge of a transparent ruler laid through the centre of the curve. In all, a complex bit of work.

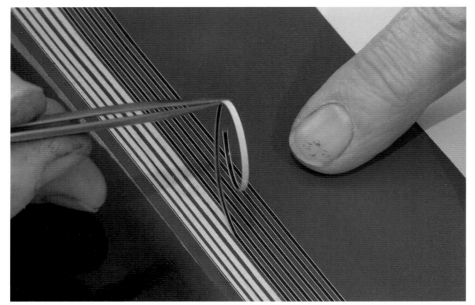

These are the LNER-style boiler bands drawn out on a sheet of waterslide transfer paper. Each band is scored on either side with a curved scalpel and then lifted with a pair of tweezers ...

... and placed around the boiler adjacent to its final position ...

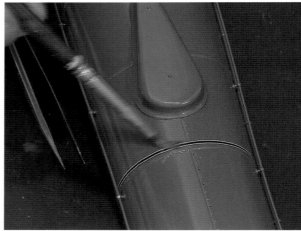

... then wetted with water by brush, but not too much water or else the adhesive will be diluted ...

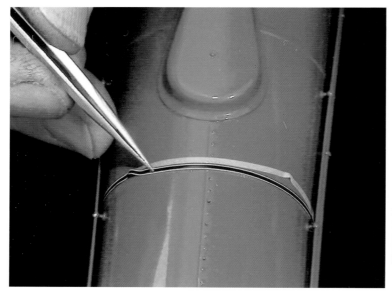

... then, after about 20 seconds, carefully teased into position ...

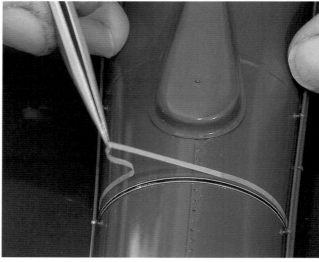

... and the backing paper removed. The transfer remains vulnerable until the adhesive is completely dry. Allow 24 hours before handling. Once dry, varnish can be carefully brushed on to seal them.

MAKING TRANSFERS

This 4mm scale, 18.83 gauge LSWR Adams Radial Tank was built by Graham Varley from the Martin Finney kit. The paint is Chris Wesson's Cellulose Drummond Green. The brown border paint was a 50/50 mix of H 19, Gloss Red and H 10, Service Brown. The boiler bands were prepared on brown-painted transfer paper and carefully cut off to give the correct 3in scale borders. The model lacks its buffers and front spectacle frames, which were fitted later by Graham.

Most lining on an engine can be applied directly with the pen but there are situations where this is impractical and other solutions need to be found. Boiler cladding bands are a particular case and cylinder covers are similar. There are other areas of an engine where direct lining is fraught with difficulty, namely – tank fronts (always), cab fronts (mostly) and tender/bunker backs (sometimes). The edge of the tank front nearer to the boiler is generally inaccessible by pen. Parts of the cab front are obscured by pipe work, safety valves, etc, and the backs of tenders can be made awkward by lamp brackets, vacuum pipes and hand rails.

In these situations a transfer may be the safest solution. Blank waterslide (decal) paper is available in a number of forms but I find the best is XtraDecal from Hannants or ATP Clear Decal from 'Airliners America' off the Web. When spraying your model, spray some of the body colour onto part of the decal sheet (50mm wide should do) but lay it on fairly thickly as the thickness of the paint is what gives the transfer its strength. Cellulose paint cannot be used for this as it is too brittle when dry. When the paint has dried, you can rule the boiler bands, or other shapes, onto it – one colour at a time, allowing ample drying time in between.

BOILER BANDS

When required for use, score each side of the band, (there is no need to cut right through) and lift off the paint together with the top veneer of paper. (If using Fox transfer paper, you will need to cut through.) Cut it to length, then position it around the boiler, brush water on it, then after about twenty seconds slide the paint strip off the paper and into position. It can be tweaked into position and pressed down with the wet brush. If there are raised bands on the model, make sure that the transfer does not overhang the edges as it will be then very vulnerable to damage and lines of colour will go missing. Also, if you haven't put the bands on straight, the transfer will accentuate the errors. If there are no raised bands on the model, you need to make sure that the transfers are all parallel and exactly at right-angles to the axis of the boiler.

If you omit or remove the formed boiler bands from the boiler, you will have much better-looking lined bands. On the prototype, the bands are just thin straps to hold the cladding in place and are only about 3/32in (2.38 mm) thick which equates to 1.2 thou (0.03 mm) in 00. In 0 gauge they are only 2.2 thou thick. You will have to rule the boiler band lining slightly under

scale to avoid overhang if there are bands on the boiler that cannot be removed. I know some etched bands are far too narrow (naming no names) and proprietary locos have them too thick and narrow to facilitate lining by brush or masking in the factory. File them off if repainting – the thickness of the transfer is quite sufficient.

In some situations the transfer will have to sit on rivets and other minor irregularities in the surface. In this case a softening solution will be required for the transfer using the precautions outlined in the Transfer Lining section.

Transfers are not the only way of lining boiler bands. The 'traditional' way was to use cigarette paper (adhesive edge only) but this restricts the length you can use so that there will be joins to be made somewhere. The other method is to use an adhesive tape, the best being Scotch 'Magic' Tape, which has a matt surface. Stick a length down to a piece of clean plastic card, glass or Formica and paint as for a transfer. For use, slice each side and then carefully lift it and try threading it under hand rails, etc, into position. I have tried it and it does work but I think it is more of a fiddle than a transfer. The problem is feeding it through narrow gaps and handling it so that it doesn't stick to itself. To feed it through a gap, stick the leading edge to a bit of thin plastic card, feed that through, then pull the tape through. That technique works with masking tape too.

Once the boiler bands are in position and have dried off, it will pay to brush on a coat of varnish to seal the edges, especially

at the ends under the boiler and at the bottom of the firebox. The boiler bands are vulnerable so they should be the last bit of lining to do.

Many awkward parts of the engine can be lined using transfers but you need to measure the part fairly precisely and draw

the outline in order to achieve accuracy with the lining. This is where planning comes in – you will, of course, have traced out the relevant parts while they were still flat!

This is an LSWR T3 No. 563 in a later guise. This Finney 7mm kit was built by Peter Kaiser for TMS Models. The lettering and garter badge were done by hand, but the numbers are from the HMRS Methfix Southern (Maunsell period) sheet. The boiler band transfers on this model are in three sections as it has raised bands. The edges of the bands were painted brown before the transfers were applied.

WASP STRIPES

A painter's nightmare. The 00 gauge model was the trial etch of the Judith Edge kit designed and built by Mike Edge. The only photographs I had to work on were a view of each side of the engine. I was perplexed by the fact that on each side the stripes went from bottom left to top right, and it took a few hours of thought before I realised that they simply wrapped over the top. All I had to do then was work out which stripe ended up where on the other side. Once that was sorted, I cut 2mm widths of black-painted waterslide paper and positioned them on the body, cutting them short at obstructions. The gaps were filled in with black paint later. The silver-painted parts are heat shields as these locomotives worked with and close to molten steel. Photos by TONY WRIGHT

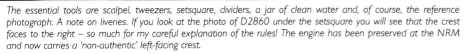

The essential tools are scalpel, tweezers, setsquare, dividers, a jar of clean water and, of course, the reference photograph. A note on liveries. If you look at the photo of D2860 under the setsquare you will see that the crest faces to the right – so much for my careful explanation of the rules! The engine has been preserved at the NRM and now carries a 'non-authentic' left-facing crest.

The ends of this shunter have been sprayed in plain yellow and a piece of plain waterslide paper has been sprayed black. With the dividers, I marked a series of dots, 2mm apart, down each side of the transfer paper and then used the marks as a guide for cutting out the strips. In fact, for this end of the loco, I only needed two strips from the A4 wide sheet. This photograph shows the first stripe (in two parts because of the door recess) in position.

All the transfer stripes are stuck on, with gaps left where there are obstructions. The order of placing the stripes generally depends on the direction of the last 45° cut made. The dividers, still set at 2mm, are used to space the stripes correctly.

The gaps in the black stripes have been filled in with a fine brush and the short stripes next to the windows have been painted on.

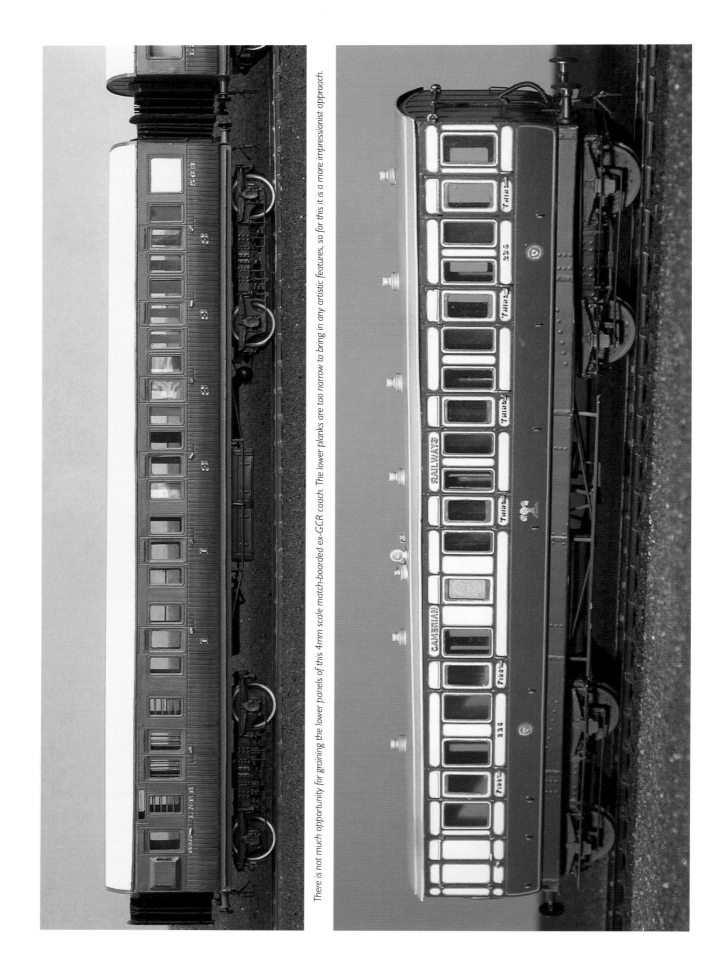

There is not much opportunity for graining the lower panels of this 4mm scale match-boarded ex-GCR coach. The lower planks are too narrow to bring in any artistic features, so for this it is a more impressionist approach.

CHAPTER SEVEN
COACHES

PAINTING

Despite having a simpler body shape than a locomotive, there are problems peculiar to coaches. The coach side is essentially a piece of flat metal with holes in, so the route you take with the spray is important so as to maintain a constant thickness of paint. One of the cardinal rules of spraying is to start and stop the spray off the edge. Window openings are surrounded by edges, but it is rather difficult to keep stopping and starting so I would advocate ignoring the openings and just continue spraying across them. This will ensure that the edges themselves receive enough paint. Do not forget to apply paint to the window reveals (the thickness of the material of the coach side); in fact it is better if these are tackled first – detail before general.

In a two-colour coach, it is usual to spray the lighter colour first, then mask off and spray the darker. If the second colour is a translucent pigment, eg in the red spectrum, the light colour underneath will remain visible for quite a few coats, so if the light colour was applied unevenly on that part of the side, there will be a patchy effect. It is best if the light colour covers the whole of the coach side.

On a panelled coach with light upper panels, the lower colour could be sprayed first and the upper panels 'flooded' with dilute paint applied by brush. You will have to experiment to find the right consistency of paint for this. The method is to introduce the dilute paint into the centre of the panel, then push the paint so that it flows as far as the raised moulding and then stops. When the brush is removed, the paint is sufficiently liquid to be self-levelling to produce a flat blemish-free surface. Do not overfill the panel or you will not have any moulding quadrant to line out (see below).

A problem with a two-colour side on a flush coach is that the ridge formed at the edge of the masking tape will interfere with the lining pen and prevent a clean line being drawn. A way round this is to put on the waist lines before the second colour goes on. Rule in the lining colours in the normal manner then, additionally, rule in adjacent to the lining a broad line of the second body colour. When completely dry, place the masking tape so that the lining is covered and the boundary is within the body colour line.

LINING

Coach lining comes in a number of styles, depending on the type of coach body. During the pregrouping period, most coach superstructures were built entirely of timber. Wooden panels were nailed to the frame of the coach and the joints where the panels butted together were protected by shaped strips of wood known as mouldings.

The rounded edge of the moulding, known as the quadrant, was where the lining was generally positioned. I say generally because there were many exceptions.

During the second decade of the twentieth century, companies started to use steel sheets to cover their coaches and, because they were no longer limited by the size of planks of wood, the steel panels were much larger so that joints and mouldings were no longer required.

Whilst the flush coaches were outnumbered by panelled ones, false panels were painted onto the flush coaches so that trains presented a uniform appearance.

The more general use of flush-sided coaches, rapidly increasing labour costs and, of course, fashion, led to simpler lining styles. In 1928 most of the railways rationalised their liveries and the Great Western took the lead, as far as coaches were concerned, by doing away with lining altogether. It did not last long, however, because it was soon reintroduced, probably because it was easier to form a straight boundary between the two colours by lining over it.

Simple lining is defined as straight lines from one end of the coach to the other. It can be one colour, as in LMS yellow, or two or three, and occasionally seven, touching lines.

The style of lining Pullman coaches was different from all the above and is dealt with in a separate section below.

The BR Blue Period actually reverted to the 'false panel' situation except that there

I think that the BR Mk I coaches were visually the best BR design, a complete train of them presenting a very uniform appearance. I remember train-spotting in the late '50s at Whitmore troughs on the WCML and seeing trains of newly-painted maroon Mk Is pulled by red Duchesses. Magic. Anyway, enough nostalgia, this is a coach I built from the Comet Models kit for my display stand. The cream paint is the same both sides, I forget which paint I used, but the crimson is Cherry 'faded crimson' on one side and Railmatch crimson on the other. Colour photos of coaches in the livery show all sorts of different reds, and paint manufacturers provide further choices. Questions in regard to this colour and its confusion with Crimson Lake crop up at intervals on Internet user groups. Crimson is effectively red with a bit of blue in it. Crimson Lake is effectively crimson with a bit of black in it. LNWR Lake is crimson with a lot of black in it. The BR Crimson and Cream style (aka Blood and Custard) was introduced in 1949 and discontinued in 1956, although there were still some coaches in the livery when the blue and grey style was introduced in 1964. The lining was gold/black above the windows and black/gold below. Non-corridor coaches were plain crimson, initially with lining, but this was dropped in about 1950. The Western Region (usual culprit) painted some non-corridor coaches in Crimson Lake with gold/black/gold waist lining, at that time, just to confuse matters. In 1956 the colour was changed to all over Crimson Lake with gold/black lining above the windows and gold/black/gold below, for all coaches.

was only one panel, around the windows, per side.

During the Sectorisation period, lining was omitted altogether but in its place came wide paint stripes.

This leaves the model painter with a number of styles to contend with –

SIMPLE LINING ON A PANELLED COACH

Simple lining on panelled coaches needs special attention to photographs, if you can find them. Have you noticed that the specialist books on liveries or coaches mostly illustrate a coach in its as–built livery and

ignore later styles? How were Cambrian corridor coaches painted in BR days? How were pregrouping coaches painted by the LNER? You will find it hard to get the information from books. You may need to trawl through the photograph dealers' stands at exhibitions to find photographs of

This 4mm scale coach is an example of the problems encountered when painting a simple lining on a panelled coach. Above the windows there is a yellow line running along the centre of each of the two mouldings. They are easy to do. The problem arises when putting the three lines of colour on the moulding under the windows. Because there was so little room on the model, I have put the upper yellow line and the black on the flat, with the lower yellow on the quadrant. This means that it has to pass over the ends of the mouldings at every door position, which means careful attention to the width of the line where it meets each obstruction. Where the pen jumps over each vertical moulding, there will inevitably be a little pool of paint which, if left, will spread out a little. This will have to be lifted with the fine spirit-damp brush.

This LNWR ex-First Class saloon in BR livery (now downgraded to Open Third) is an example of a panelled coach painted in a simple lined livery. It has no lining above the windows, but below the windows the lining is level with the door handles. This makes for a very awkward masking situation, as you would be bound to get leaks adjacent to each moulding. I think I would be tempted to place the masking along the waist beading and fill in the crimson above it from the pen as a broad line. I think these older coaches are fascinating; this one has had panels replaced with tongue-and-groove boards; others were partly sheeted over. You never see them modelled, do you?

Photo by T. J. EDGINGTON

the vehicle in the required livery, to find where the lining was positioned. My copy of *LMS Coaches* by Jenkinson and Essery, despite being a comprehensive history, contains not one photograph of an LMS panelled coach in the LMS simple livery.

The only railways to use this style were the LMS, GWR and BR. The LMS and GWR tended to line on the mouldings, but BR mostly centred the waist-line level with the door handles, which puts the lining in the centre of the waist panel (which also makes it very difficult to mask the cream from the crimson). The position of the lining above the windows in BR livery depended on the style of the coach and the whim of the painter and on high window stock it was omitted altogether.

The waist-line moulding on etched coaches, especially older kits, can be a bit narrow or even irregular, which will make it difficult to get the two or three colours in place. Here again it is difficult to find photographs that show how the real coach lining was arranged in the simpler styles. Either or both of the gold lines will need to be on the quadrant but, of course, being a straight line, they have to cross over the junctions of vertical panelling. A cheat would be to put the upper gold line on top of the moulding adjacent to the black but put the lower gold line on the quadrant where there are fewer vertical mouldings.

Because the moulding is narrow and the gold lines are hopping over the junctions with the vertical panelling, it would be a

This 7mm scale GWR clerestory brake third that I built for Paul Jones is from the Slater's kit. It is painted in the 1928–34 style with simple gold/black waist lining and black shadow line under the eaves. The body side paint is all PP but the underframe was painted in my usual 'dirty' mix. I weathered the coach on Martyn Welch principles. ('Clerestory', by the way, is pronounced Clear-storey, not Kler-ess-tree.)

Photographs of this type of kitchen car (diagram 1697) must be exceedingly rare as I have not seen one, nor has my customer. The general theory of LMS coach lettering is that the 'LMS' and the number share the same vertical centre line as the panel immediately above the waist line, if you follow. Similarly, the crest is centred on either the panel or the vertical lining nearest the centre of the coach. The 'Kitchen' and 'Car' are equally spaced from the crest. There were variations of course! The model is to 7mm scale, built by Graham Varley who will glaze it and add the gangways.

This is a flush-sided period III coach, so the first stage here is to rule in all the straight gold lines ...

... and then fill in all the corners carefully with a fine brush. This is followed with the vermilion lines each side of the gold, and finally the black infill. Flush coaches are more difficult to do in the fully-lined style, as there are no guides for the corners.

brave man who attempted using transfer lining for this style on anything other than BR. A pen, be it bow or tube, is the only way.

SIMPLE LINING ON A FLUSH COACH

Although this is the simplest form of coach lining, there will be obstacles, such as door and commode handles, door stops and hinges that may prevent a continuous line. If these cannot be left off until after painting, then you will just have to make the best of it and use the remedial techniques to remove any blemishes as the pen is continually removed and replaced. If lining with a pen, lines can be continued under commode handles with careful use of the brush.

If you haven't yet built up your pen skills, this style lends itself to waterslide transfers. Coach lining was bright and brash, like transfers, and they can be easily fed under commode handles. The difficulty is keeping the line straight when it has to be cut into many pieces.

FALSE PANELS ON A FLUSH-SIDED COACH

Full lining on a flush coach was applied by LMS, GWR and SR. Start with all the horizontal lining. You will need to support the ruler off the surface when doing the

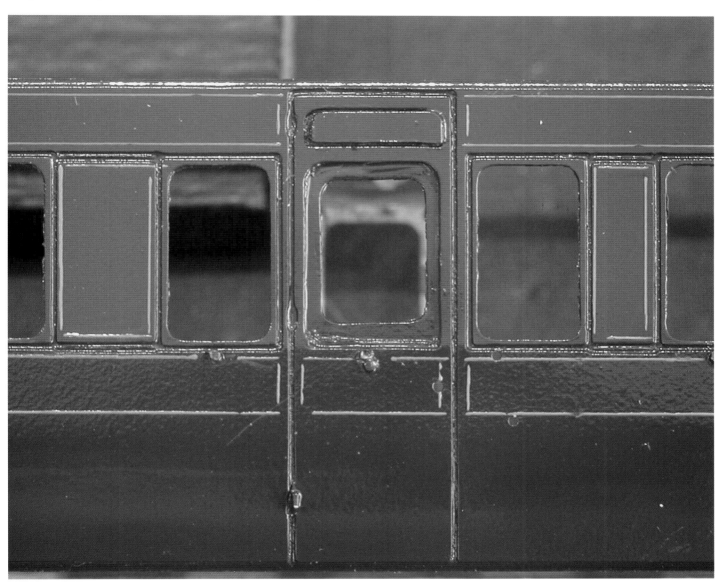

This 4mm scale Maunsell coach was a 'lining-only' commission. The first stage for a flush-sided coach is to rule in the straight lines; in this case the lining colour is a chrome orange for which I used H9, Tan.

The second stage is to fill in the corners with a brush ...

And the third and fourth are to repeat the process with the black line. This is very often omitted from coaches I have seen on exhibition layouts. It does make a difference. I have painted in the undercoat for the droplights, which were a natural wood finish. It pays to be careful with the solder when fixing the droplights, as a ragged boundary between the two colours is difficult to disguise.

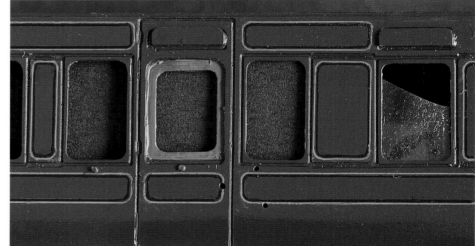

The coach was finished with Methfix transfers. One slight problem was the location of the 'Southern Railway'. Before the introduction of the high-window stock, the 'SR' was placed in the upper panels. On the corridor side of this coach the windows are high, so the 'SR' goes in the waist panels, but what about this side? I could not find any photos of the compartment side. All my books have SR official photographs which seem to have been only of the corridor side; I presume it was deemed more 'modern'.

vertical lines so as not to smudge the horizontals. Try to draw the lines to the right length so as to limit the amount of cutting back required for forming the corners. This is more important for the Southern style where you have less opportunity to make corrections with a second colour. On LMS and GWR the centre of the moulding is black, which can be used to overpaint errors on one side of the gold. On the Southern there was a black line inside the orange but on a 4mm model it is barely visible and not really useful for correcting errors, which generally occur on the outsides of corners.

A particularly difficult livery is the full LMS gold/vermilion/black style. There are seven lines of colour on each moulding (v/g/v/b/v/g/v), which makes it over 1,000 corners to be brushed in per coach. Yes, I have two customers who require this level of detail in both 4mm and 7mm scales. Understandably, this livery is usually simplified to g/b/g in non-museum standard models.

PANELLED LINING ON A PANELLED COACH

This style is not actually as daunting as it sounds unless you are doing that pre-1910 GW style. The lighter of the lining colours was generally gold or a look-alike, such as ochre, depending on the affluence of the company or period. This was placed on the quadrant, not the flat top of the moulding (the Southern was an exception, as the quadrant was black and the orange line sat on the moulding).

In the model, an etching has a concave edge and plastic will have a square edge to the mouldings, so it is not possible to exactly replicate prototype practice. If you hold the pen at a very low angle to the coach side, it is possible to rule a line along the upstand of the moulding, but your paint should be fairly thick so that it does not run back onto the panel. You do not need a ruler for this task. The difficulty is going around the corners as it is hard to turn the

The mouldings which covered and protected the joints in the boards that formed the 'panels' of the coach sides had a simple quadrant planed on the edges. All the decorative lining that the various companies used was mostly placed on the moulding, and rarely on the panel. The flat of the moulding was painted either in the panel colour, or the lower panel colour if that was different (eg LNWR), or black. The only exception to that would be a very narrow moulding lined down the centre, such as used by the GNR and LNER. The most common lining colour for the quadrant was gold or a look-alike such as ochre, but the Southern used black. The LMS lining illustrated was the most complex of the Big Four and, surprisingly, it survived the rationalisations of 1928. Non-gangwayed coaches had yellow instead of gold. The red was vermilion, on the cusp between red and orange. If replicating this livery on a model, the normal rule of reducing the intensity of lining colours does not apply, as a less bright red would not show up against the crimson lake.

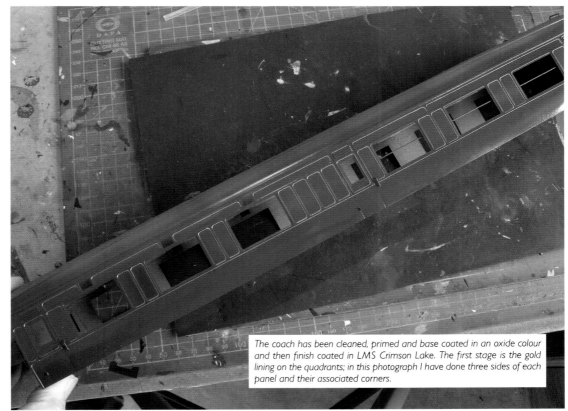

The coach has been cleaned, primed and base coated in an oxide colour and then finish coated in LMS Crimson Lake. The first stage is the gold lining on the quadrants; in this photograph I have done three sides of each panel and their associated corners.

PROTOTYPE LINING ON COACH MOULDINGS

Fig. 3 – LMS COACH LINING (1923–1933)

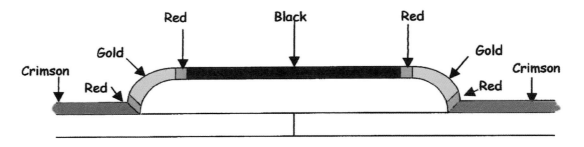

Fig. 4 – GWR COACH LINING (1923–1928)

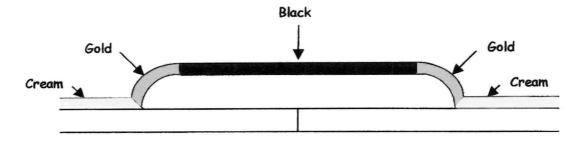

Fig. 5 – LNER COACH LINING

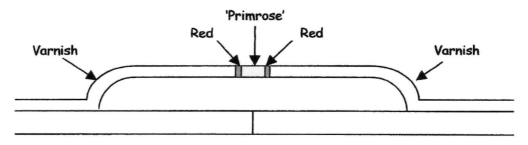

Fig. 6 – SR COACH LINING (1923–1936)

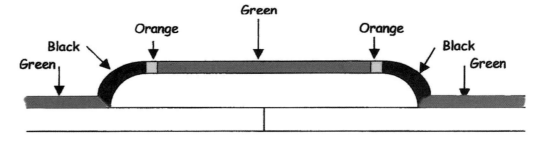

ETCHED MODEL LINING

Fig. 7 – LMS COACH LINING

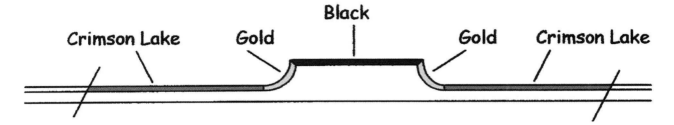

Fig. 8 – GWR COACH LINING

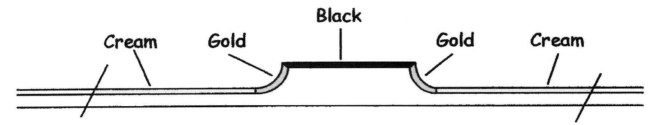

Fig. 9 – LNER COACH LINING

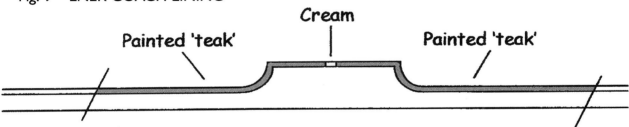

Fig. 10 – SR COACH LINING

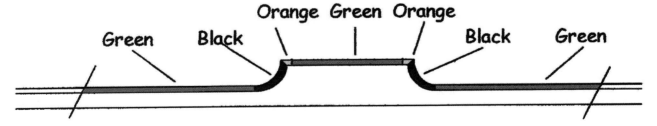

The convex quadrant of the mouldings never appears in small-scale models. In etched brass it is concave, as illustrated here, and in plastic, either kits or scratchbuilt, it is nearly square. Lining the model is invariably a compromise, principally due to the skill of the person holding the pen, but also due to the different shape of the mouldings. The 'quadrant' can be coloured in with a bow pen held almost flat so that the outside of the lower blade rests on the panel, or on a ruler used as a rest. The lining schemes shown here represent a minimum, although some would argue that the black of the Southern style could be omitted, and it usually is.

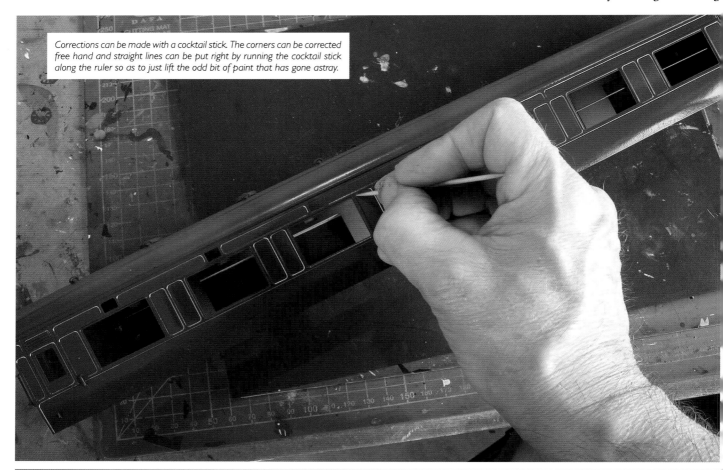

Corrections can be made with a cocktail stick. The corners can be corrected free hand and straight lines can be put right by running the cocktail stick along the ruler so as to just lift the odd bit of paint that has gone astray.

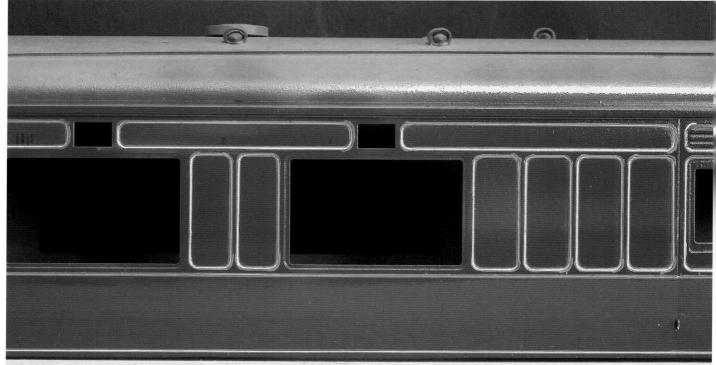

The vermilion lines have been drawn each side of the gold, the outer one on top of the moulding and the inner on the panel. The outer lines are a little untidy but I can overpaint these with the black to bring them back into line.

pen at such an angle. It is possible to start from the mid point of one corner and finish on the mid point of the next so that when you turn the coach through 90° you can pick it up and continue the line.

The procedure is to do all the lines in one direction, working from top to bottom, turn the coach, repeat for the verticals on one side of the panels, turn again, do the other side of the horizontals, turn again and finish the verticals. After this some lining will have to be completed by brush, especially the round-ended waist panels and

adjacent to the door key holes. When this colour is finished, use the white spirit damp brush to tidy everything up until the lines are perfect. Put the coach away to dry for a couple of days.

The second lining colour can then be applied on top of the mouldings to finish off. This is best done by drawing the outline first with pen and ruler, allowing this to dry, then filling in between with either pen or brush, depending on the width to fill. In small scales a couple of strokes with the pen will fill in a simple panel moulding,

but adjacent to the doors, the distance between the quadrants will be greater, plus the fact that door hinges and handles, etc, will prevent the pen from drawing a smooth line, so here brush infill is probable. The trouble with using the brush, is that the paint will go down thinner than when applied by pen, so a second coat may be necessary.

Coach lining does not have the same set of problems as locomotive painting; there are no odd shapes and no large-radius curved lining, but any coach before 1933

The first stage of painting the centres of the mouldings in black is to rule in the straight edges ...

... and then fill in between with a brush. This stage usually requires two coats and great care brushing in the corners. This coach has about 65 panels, 260 panel corners each with four colours in the lining – that's a total of 1,040 corners to paint in!

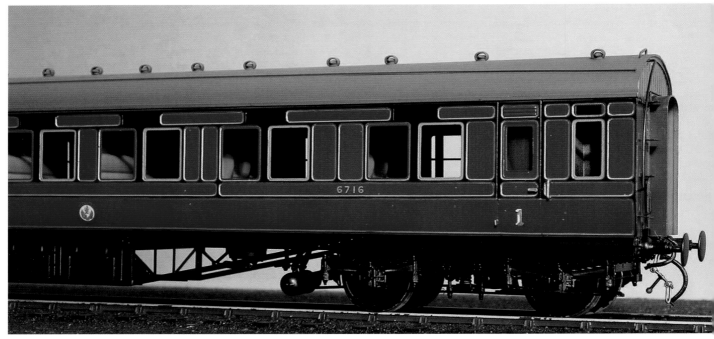

The coach was completed by painting the fixed window frames in a natural wood colour, masking off and painting the roof in H67 matt grey, applying Methfix transfers and varnishing in gloss satin. The coach was then returned to the builder, Graham Varley, for glazing and finishing.

had a lot of lining. If your coach has, say, 35 panels each side, that is 70 panels in total, each of which has four corners. That is 280 corners to do per colour – if anything is going to test your patience, this is it. There is no advice I can give to make the task easier except allow yourself plenty of time, work to a system, and if you do start to make lots of mistakes on the lining, walk away from it. However, you must get back to it to correct the errors before the lining paint has set hard.

Droplight frames and window frames (bolections) were sometimes left in their natural wood colour, mahogany in some schemes (eg GWR) and a lighter wood colour in others, (Midland, early LMS and SR). The GWR mahogany is generally represented by a maroon colour in the model and, in fact, became maroon in the later years of the GW. Rule a line around the outside of the frame and apply the remainder of the colour by brush. If you are really careful, it is possible to lay the pen on its side so that the paint comes out of the side gap and effectively draws a very broad line the width of the frame. This generally saves having to do a second coat to build up the colour density but it is a risky process.

A sample programme for the painting of an LNWR or pre-1928 GWR chocolate and cream coach would be —

Day 1. Clean, check and prime.

Day 2. Apply the lighter body colour. Two coats may be needed, which may be possible for enamels in the same day if you start early enough.

Day 3. Mask off carefully and apply the darker body colour. Remove masking.

Day 4. Side 1. Rule in the quadrant colour. Rule in the edges and then paint ventilators with a brush, carefully.

Day 5. Side 1. Rule in outlines of the moulding colour, droplights and the edges of any bolections.

Day 6. Side 1. Infill mouldings, etc. Lining on ventilators.

Day 7 – 9. Repeat 4 – 6 for side 2.

Day 10. Touching up – yes, this will be necessary. Fitting hand rails, etc.

Day 11. Lettering, etc. This could be a nice easy day except for putting on tiny numbers four times per coach. Varnish.

Day 12. Glazing, reassemble and admire.

The above does not take into account painting and fitting interiors. Ideally, if using enamel paint, a week would be nice between day 2 and day 3. If you have more than one coach to do, the total time will depend on how much of the day you can spare to work on them. If you have to get a train of coaches ready for an exhibition and are running late – start sooner!

BR BLUE PERIOD

The BR blue/grey is a simplified form of false panel lining. Only one colour in the lining but it forms a complete panel by turning up at the ends and has rounded corners. To avoid the problems of having to line along a masking ridge, spray the grey colour first, without masking. Line around the panel in white, then, when that is dry, line outside that in blue. Finally, mask off in the manner described above and then spray the remainder in blue. If you have square-cornered masking, there will be some touching-up to do at the rounded corners. To avoid this, carefully cut the masking corners to match the curve or make a 45° cut across the corners and fill with Maskol.

SECTORISATION

During the Sectorisation period, lining was dropped from coach liveries and blocks of colour became the norm. The painting of these is an exercise in masking and working out a way of minimising it. I have not done much of this style as, because there is no lining or large areas of paint, most people can do their own – or simply rely on ready-to-run stock.

My sole example for illustration is the Hornby-Dublo brake third done up as an InterCity buffet car. The first paint on was the white stripe under the windows, sprayed without masking. The white was masked with tape cut to size, using the base of the windows to achieve a straight line with the tape. Next on were the two

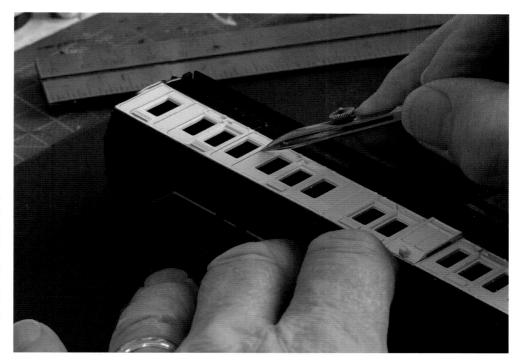

These coaches were built from the M&L kits. The LNW coaches I built at the time followed the sequence – spray white, mask, spray dark lake, lining ochre, fill in mouldings, bolections, droplights and ventilators in dark lake (twice) and then finally line the ventilators. This sequence of photographs (unfortunately on different coaches) shows the lining process. To get the paint to lie on the side of the moulding, the pen is held as flat as possible, with the bottom blade in contact with the panel. This will keep the line straight without need of a ruler.

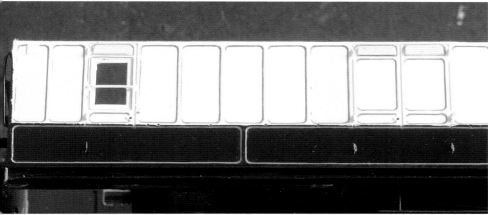

The second photograph shows the ochre lining completed and the corners tidied up.

Finally, the mouldings are filled up by ruling on the paint in a series of touching lines, starting with the edges and filling in. The corners will have to be brushed and, as the dark lake is not a particularly strong pigment, will probably have to be done twice. The bolections and droplights can be done by ruling in the edge then laying the pen on its side to fill in the remainder. The ventilators are usually a fiddle as, because of the ridges, it is difficult to get a clean edge, so some paint lifting will be required.

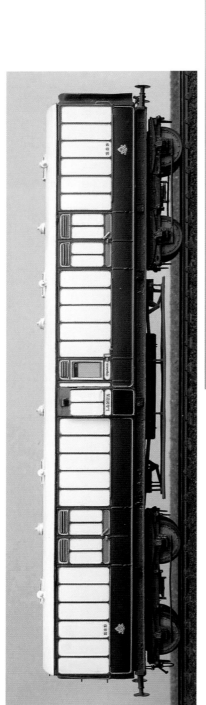

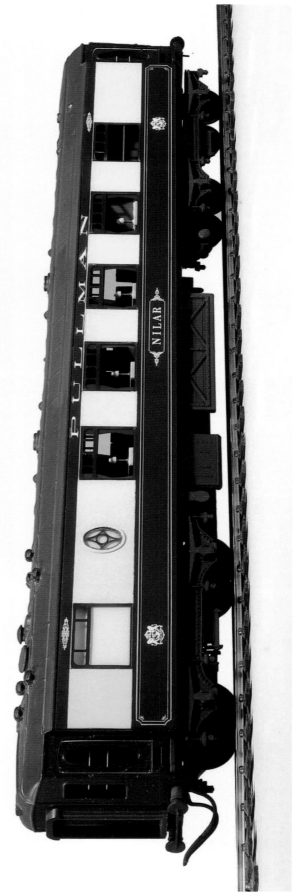

patches of red. The lower red stripe was masked with tape that defined the lower edge of the stripe but overlapped onto the white masking, which was left in place. The upper red stripe was also masked with a cut-to-length strip. The next colour was the beige, sprayed without further masking. The lower patch of beige was masked by tape that overlapped onto the red masking. The upper beige masking was overlapped onto the upper red masking. Finally, the dark grey was sprayed onto the window section.

The points to note are that, apart from the first piece of tape that has to be cut to a precise width, all the other masking is defining one edge only. This simplifies matters. However, tape is remaining in place throughout the painting process, so we have to make sure that paint is thoroughly dry before masking the next stage and that tape edges are well stuck down. The downside is that any cock-ups will not be discovered until the masking is finally removed, just after the dark grey has been sprayed.

PULLMANS

Pullman cars present a unique set of problems, as the colour distribution and lining are quite different from other companies. The cars are effectively umber with a series of rectangular cream panels between the windows. The lining differs in extent, depending on the era, but mainly consists of simple straight horizontal lines, straight vertical lines with arrow heads or, in the lower panels, rococo curlicues.

The roof can either be painted first or left until the rest is complete. If done first, mask it off when dry, but make sure that the edges are well bedded down as this masking will be in place while both the cream and the umber are applied to the sides and ends. Next paint the cream between the windows (and above if doing the white Pullmans). When this is dry, carefully measure and cut the masking to cover the cream areas, leaving the correct space adjacent to the windows for the umber areas. The umber is next. Take care that all surfaces around the windows are covered with paint, as it is very easy to forget the reveals. The roof masking should now be removed before the body is put aside to dry.

One of the problems with Pullmans is the lack of detailed photographs, as the lining is difficult to see in the cream areas. There are a number of authentically painted preserved cars around, so seek them out

and take your own photos. One of my reference photographs was taken from an advert in the *Radio Times!*

Most of the lining is simple, it is only the main panel and the name cartouche that include the curly bits. Luckily, there are transfers for these and the little filigree lozenges that sit in the eaves panel. I normally use the Methfix transfers for these complications but unfortunately the 4mm scale ones have been discontinued. There are Pressfix and waterslide varieties available. Set out and apply the curly bits and then, when dry, draw the joining horizontal lines with a pen.

TEAK AND WOOD FINISHES

This section of a teak coach was photographed so that the print came out at roughly 7mm scale. The coach was a long-term resident at Bewdley on the Severn Valley Railway, while being renovated and modified for wheelchair use. It represents a well-aged teak, probably much darker than service stock was in LNER days. It is a very difficult colour to capture, as it is virtually impossible to establish what a train of teak coaches looked like when fairly new.

Most of the 'teak' finishes I have seen on exhibition layouts are based on some fantasy existing in the mind of the painter. Impressionism extrapolated to the point of Abstract.

To get an approximation of the teak effect requires two things, firstly a clear photograph of the original, and then secondly, the techniques required to imitate that on the model.

There are numerous teak coaches on our preserved railways; the Severn Valley and North York Moors each have a whole train of them, but there are many other vehicles dotted around the country.

WORKING FROM PHOTOS

Right, select your vehicle and photograph a section of it broadside on. Not just any old photo but a 'measured' one. I will explain. Ideally, the print you are going to copy will be to the same scale as your model so that you can get an impression of just how

visible the grain is, as well as an approximate indication of the colour. Let us suppose that your print is going to be the usual 6in x 4in. 6in at 7mm scale is 21ft 9in and at 4mm scale it is about 38ft. So, if you model in 7mm scale, measure 21ft 9in of the coach, then make a mental note of where that is on the coach side or place a marker on the ground, then position yourself so that that amount of the coach side fills your viewfinder frame. Photograph the whole coach side in sections. For other scales or print sizes, lay your scale rule alongside your real world rule and simply read off the equivalent lengths you will need to fill the frame.

The prints will now be to your scale and you will be able to see just how many of the surface features are visible, and require translation. At this stage you could simply cut the prints up and paste them on your coach side – but that would be cheating.

The whole of this 7mm scale LNER Thompson Full Brake was sprayed in a gloss buff and that was allowed to dry thoroughly before the graining coat was brushed on. In this photograph the first panel has had its bottom edge tidied up. The second is fully brushed out. The masking of the roof is still in place despite my advocating that it should be removed; there is a reason for this. I had used a cellulose paint for the white roof so it needed to be done before the enamel sides. The white roof is prone to marking so I left the masking on for protection. Note that the newspaper has been folded with a pleat along its centre to allow for the roof ventilators.

The chisel-pointed cocktail stick has been drawn along the boundary line between the vertical and horizontal graining ...

... and the lower part cleaned off. There are still some traces of brown paint in the lower panels and the line is not too clean where the door bumpers prevent the cocktail stick being drawn through the paint.

Alternate panels should mean alternate panels. You can see here that I have ignored my own rules as I have treated the double doors as a single panel. Wrong.

PAINTING

Now for the painting. I am assuming that you have gone through the cleaning process and the priming and not just skipped to this point in the book, missing out the really important bits. Make sure the surface is smooth. Spray on an equally smooth coat of base colour, which, for teak, will be an ochre colour for a newish vehicle or more of a tan for an older one, preferably gloss. You can use P995 'Teak base coat'. For mahogany use an orangey shade. The base coat should be consistent – just because it is to be covered with the graining coat doesn't mean it can be patchy. When you've painted the model, spray the same paint onto some scrap for a practice piece.

The tricky bit is the graining, and this is where the photos are essential. You do not need to imitate all the idiosyncrasies of the grain pattern, choose one of the simpler panels and copy that. If you are painting a steel vehicle in ersatz teak, you do not have to imitate teak, but you do have to imitate a painter imitating teak. The difference between the two is that the painter will have used only base coat and a one or two colour graining coat whereas real wood grain will be multi coloured (although in

practical terms only one or two extra colours are needed on a model).

The basic graining colour can be either P997 Golden Teak, P996 Weathered Teak top coat or any chestnut brown colour, again for a young vehicle – I use H133 Satin Brown or add some umber for an older one. I put some in a 1oz. jam jar then add a couple of drops of linseed oil and quite a few drops of white spirit. I know this sounds vague but I never measure – it's a case of let's see how it goes, then add a bit more of this or that. Brush some on to the practice piece and start graining to see how things are behaving and whether the general colour balance is ok.

What we have created in the jar is a 'scumble'. Scumble is defined as a translucent coating or an opaque coating applied very thinly so as to become translucent. Decorators who wish to produce a wood grain finish will use commercially produced scumble such as Ratcliffe's, which is a well-known make. A problem with commercial scumble is that it is designed to take a long time to dry so that painters working in the real world have time to produce the grain patterns on large areas.

THE GRAINING

When brushed out, the scumble will not initially form a grain, it will be just an amorphous layer of thick and thin paint. It can be brushed quite randomly onto the panel; you don't need to get this coat consistent. What happens now is that the white spirit will start to evaporate out quite quickly, drying the paint. At this point take up a reasonable soft-bristled, second division paint brush and brush out the paint in the direction of the grain. With a bit of luck you will now see the grain beginning to form as the brush bristles pass through the paint layer and expose the base coat. If the paint hasn't dried enough, the gaps will close up again and you will have to wait a little longer and then repeat. As the paint reaches the right degree of dryness the grain will stay.

As the paint continues to dry, other effects can be introduced. The grain can be 'smudged' by dragging the brush across the grain and then brushing along the grain again lightly over the top. Flares (features that occur at right-angles to the grain) can be imitated by scratching across the grain with a cocktail stick and then smudging by rebrushing along the grain. I hope this is

This shows the effects that can be achieved with a simple two-colour system using the method described in the text to create the graining. For a wooden coach, one or two additional colours can be used to create more subtle effects, the emphasis being on subtle.

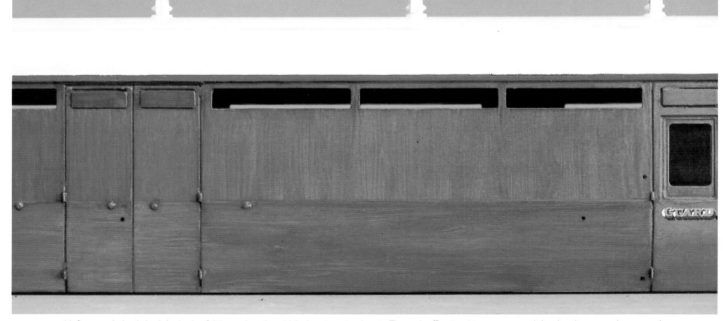

Unfortunately, I only had the body of this coach so I couldn't show it on its chassis. The teak effect is a bit messy around the door bumpers; there must be a moral there. Transfers are again by Methfix. The gutter was painted a solid colour (good old H9), to match the graining.

clear. A whorl can be produced by brushing an elliptical shape while the mix is comparatively wet, then when the workability is reduced, brush along the grain over the area. Eyes around knots can be introduced by giving the brush a wiggle and then a wiggle the opposite way in the adjacent stroke.

FLUSH COACHES

The grain painted onto a steel coach (LNER style) will be vertical from the gutter to a line through the bottom of the windows. Below that it will be horizontal. Depending on the type of coach, the horizontal panels may have mock joints.

Start with the vertical grain between two windows, making sure that the graining continues below the base level of the windows so that the whole area is grained. Take a cocktail stick, cut off the point, then cut a chisel point on the blunt end. Take a ruler, place it along the horizontal/vertical graining division, then run the cocktail stick chisel point, broadside on, through the paint. Hopefully, this will create a clean straight lower boundary to the vertically-grained panel. Any paint below this should be carefully cleaned off completely with white spirit and paper towel. Repeat for each of the upper panels. Put aside for a day.

The lower panels are more difficult. They are longer so you will have to work more quickly. Also there will be vertical boundaries in the shape of door panels or mock joints. Tackle alternate panels, cleaning off any overruns after defining the boundaries with a cocktail stick as above. A day later fill in the remaining panels, masking off the existing paint if you wish.

The coach will therefore take six days to finish (three days each side). If you are feeling confident (or rash) it can be done quicker.

PANELLED COACHES

With panelled coaches there are well defined boundaries – the beading – between panels, which, unfortunately, create a further set of problems. The base coat of your preferred colour is sprayed on just the same, to give a smooth surface. The problems occur when brushing out the grain. As the brush approaches the beading at the end of the stroke, it will be lifted off the surface by the beading so that adjacent to the beading there will be a blank, ungrained area. If you try to brush backwards from this end to get graining close to the beading, there will be an untidy

I built this little 4mm scale van from the D&S kit some years ago. It is painted in the Cherry Paints teak system – base coat and either 'Golden Teak' or 'Weathered Teak'. This is the golden variety. In those days I thinned the top coat with varnish for graining, which was fine for a coach with small panels, but it dried rather too quickly to grain a large panel. There being no transfers for 'Parcels, Fruit and Milk', I had to attempt them by hand.

area where the graining from the two directions meets up. What I do is slow down as I approach the beading at the end of the stroke and at the same time lift the brush into a more vertical position so that the bristles stay in contact with the wet paint for as long as possible. I then brush the next line of grain in the opposite direction.

On GNR/LNER style coaches, the grain, on any piece of panelling, always ran parallel to the longer side.

Paint will collect on the beading, so it will have to be carefully brushed out along the beading. Any paint that goes over the beading and on to the next panel will need to be cleaned off. Ideally, you will grain alternate panels and come back to the intermediate panels once the first set is dry.

The graining on wooden coaches will naturally be more complex than that painted onto a steel coach. On prototype steel coaches, the painter would apply varnish after the first graining coat, and then add a second graining coat to give depth. I am not saying that you need to apply this additional layer of varnish, but a second graining coat, applied more thinly than the first, will add to the character of the grain, especially if it is a subtle mix of hues. Use the practice piece to experiment on secondary colour effects. Be subtle.

For more sophistication in the graining, you will need a palette to enable you to mix two or more additional colours at random. It need not be bought specially, I just use glazed card. You will need to experiment to find the colours for your particular vehicle, but for a start try tan, umber, dark green, red oxide and chrome orange, available variously from the Humbrol and Precision ranges. These colours mixed together in various pro-

portions will produce the hues present in natural wood. They can be applied as the first graining coat or as a thinner, second graining over the first – once it has properly dried out. It is essential that your first graining layers are completely dry before any enhancement is added so that, and I repeat it yet again, alterations can be made without destroying your initial work.

There was an interesting article on teak graining, using tinted wood varnishes, by Martin Welch in *MRJ* No. 176. I haven't used that method, but it looks like it's worth a try. Interestingly, that issue's 'Portfolio' picture was a locomotive that I lined, but the gem is that on the opposite page, a photograph of a coach grained by Dave Studley. That is the standard to aim for.

Getting a good teak effect is a slow painstaking process. It is certainly not the 'prod with a stiff brush' approach I have seen described in magazine articles and on Internet user groups.

LINING

The lining on LNER or GNR coaches sits in the centre of the beading. All the lower panel beading is lined, but in the upper panels, only the vertical beading (providing that it is not adjacent to a window or door), is lined. The upper beading lining ends in diamond-shaped 'arrow heads' at each end of the line. In the LNER style, the lining is 'primrose' edged in red. This can be represented by lining in red and then, when dry, lining over the top with a slightly narrowed pen so that the red just peeps through at the sides. H No. 7 can be used for primrose. In GNR days, the edging was blue. I know it is hardly visible but if you put a GNR coach by an LNER one you can see the difference.

COACH INTERIORS

Once the roof is on and the coach is glazed, the interior is quite difficult to see, so the lengths you go to to detail the interior is a matter of personal requirements.

Up until now I have stressed the use of gloss paints for the exterior of stock but inside they are not necessary, and for upholstery absolutely forbidden. If you are painting the seat upholstery, use a dead matt paint, you can add extra matting agent if required.

Ideally, you will have set foot inside a restored coach, or a real one if modelling the current scene, and photographed the detail before you start work. How much of the detail you propose to reproduce is up to you, but knowing what to miss out is better than not knowing what should be there. Coach interior paint schemes are poorly documented so a visit to a preserved coach may be necessary. Coach restorers, working at the Cinderella end of the preservation scene, tend to be quite zealous and try to get things right. Because the interiors were not open to the elements, the earliest layers of paint are usually still intact underneath the later paint schemes so they can make a fair stab at the right colour.

There are some great opportunities in these days of PCs and photographic manipulation software to photograph the interiors of coaches and then reproduce them in a form that can be simply stuck inside our models. This would be a very good way of representing upholstery patterns.

I have recently built a pair of LSBSCR Driving Trailers which had tram-type

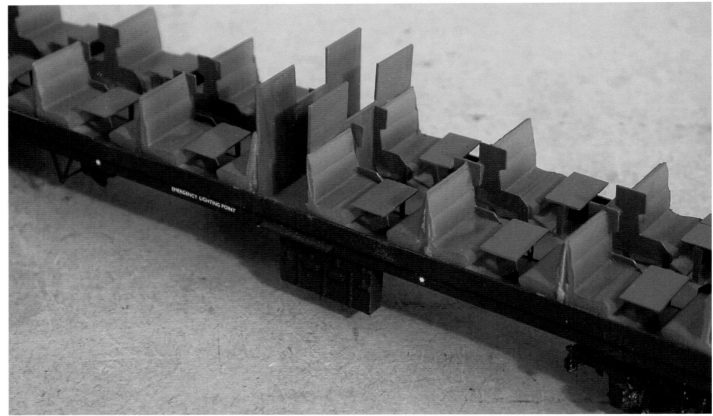

This is the interior of a 4mm Comet BR Mk.I that I built and painted some 16 years ago – a bit crude by my present standards. The whole of the assembly, constructed from Comet parts mounted on a sheet of plastic card, was painted with aerosol red oxide primer to give the seats a matt 'rusty red' colour that seems to be a favourite colour for third class seating. The wooden partitions, seat ends and tables were simply given basic graining with GWR Chocolate over the oxide. The close-up of the outside of the coach shows that little of the interior is really visible in this scale.

reversible seats in rattan. It just happens that we have a rattan window seat, so I photographed the fabric and put the results through my photo editing software.

For those who are familiar with photo editing, the rest is simply a matter of scaling down the image and then copying and pasting until an A4 sheet is filled or there are enough images for the job. The scaling is a bit hit and miss, so you may have to resort to measuring the printed image and comparing it to the dimensions of the seat. Don't worry too much about it, it's an impression we are after. Print out onto plain paper, cut it up and stick it on.

If you do not have access to this technology, then the only option is to paint the seats in a plain colour, once you have done the research to find out what it should be.

The timing of painting the interior depends on how much of it is fixed as part of the general construction. The partitions may have to be soldered in as part of the strength of the vehicle or they may be part of a floor unit that is slipped in later. The seats can always be painted separately and glued in later. If the interior walls are

grained, it is best to follow the methods for teak – spray on the base coat then brush the graining, although there is no point imitating any intricate graining patterns nor doing more than one graining coat. The base coat, and plain colour walls, should be

sprayed before the exterior is painted. Don't forget to mask inside the windows.

If you are building the coach interior furnishings from scratch, i.e. using plastic card, it will pay to use black card to avoid having to touch up glaring white edges.

This recently constructed coach interior takes full advantage of today's photo technology. The rattan seats are photographically produced, printed on plain paper and stuck to the plastic card seat with Humbrol Liquid Poly. The sepia carriage prints could have been produced in the same way but in this instance it was quicker to paint them.

Of all the major pre-grouping railways, the livery of the coaching stock of the LBSC seems to be the least well documented. I uncovered the following vague references in different publications – (1) all over brown, (2) umber lined in yellow and black, and (3) umber relieved with orange lines. I opted for ochre for the lining, mixed 60% H9 Tan and 40% H69 Gloss Yellow. Secondary passenger locos were lined in ochre, so I assumed that the coaches would be no different. (Express passenger locos and the principal coaches were lined in gold leaf during the Umber period.) There should be lining around the droplights but there is a level of panelling missing, so there was nothing to put the lining on. The lettering is in gold with black shading, for which there are no transfers available, so I brushed on faint letters in ochre and then over painted in P984 Brass. Metallic paints are more difficult to lift and remove as they tend to smear, so I attended to the 'size, shape and spacing' with a more readily removable paint.

CHAPTER EIGHT
WAGONS

By the time you have read this far, you will realise that there is nothing to add to the painting techniques, so far described, in order to paint wagons.

The difficulty with wagons is the lettering. Hand lettering is covered in that section. Model wagons are traditionally painted in matt paints which will lead to problems when lettering, either by hand or transfer. Hand lettering alterations and corrections can spread the letter colour into the matt paint but this can be covered by overpainting with the body colour in the area. Waterslide and rub-down transfers do not stick well to matt paint, so it would pay to use a more glossy paint or brush on some gloss varnish in the areas to take transfers. The whole can be matted down with a

final coat of matt varnish. The only thing peculiar to wagons is that they present quite a lumpy surface on which to apply transfers. Bolts, straps and steel sections are present on the surface, and, in the case of plastic ready-to-run stock, are sometimes exaggerated. If you are trying to get a transfer to lie across a gross surface feature, cut out the section of transfer that is impeded and fit the remaining parts in their correct position on the flat. When dry, paint in the missing bit on the projecting parts.

Another problem with wagons is their colour. This is the subject of endless Internet correspondence, more even than the colour of BR Crimson. Although wagons were the principal revenue earner for the railway company, their paintwork was

purely protective. In the main, the exterior was grey or a version of brown. The grey was white lead with a bit of black in it and the brown was red lead with a bit of black in it. Each railway may have had a formula for mixing, but it was all very rough and ready and as soon as they entered traffic it all started to fade and get dirty.

It is only in recent years that strictly specified colours have been used, and these, too, weather down.

When I see photographs of preserved freight trains, I think they all look very unnatural, especially uniformly painted steel mineral wagons. I think that all freight vehicles on a model railway should be weathered. It is their natural state. Only locomotives and coaches were cleaned.

The Midland open is a Slater's plastic model, again brush painted and lettered with Slater's spirit fix transfers provided in the kit.

I haven't built, or painted, a wagon for about 20 years, so these photos represent a quite simple approach to painting. Although not weathered, they each had the face of the wheels and parts of the undergear painted with the erstwhile Humbrol 'Track Colour'; what a useful paint that was. Also each was finished with a spray of 'dirty thinners' to take off the gleam from the white lettering. They are to 4mm scale, 18.2 mm gauge. The LNWR wagon is from D & S models in whitemetal, brush painted with Precision LNW Wagon Grey. The transfers are from the Methfix LNW wagon sheet.

The Great Northern van is another whitemetal kit from D & S. As there were no GN transfers available, I used a 'G' from the Methfix GWR sheet and modified its shape with paint to the GN style. The 'N' came from the LNER sheet. All these years it has been stored, in ex-works paintwork (matt brown), but I decided to try out a 'quick fix' weathering technique that I timed, start to finish, on one side and one end. On a palette I mixed a brushful of H33 Matt Black and two or three of white spirit. This was painted over the wagon superstructure, making sure it was all covered. I then cleaned out the brush and started brushing the dilute paint off the model. A lot went into the corners and cracks and stayed there, but the flatter areas were cleared of most of the black, revealing more of the brown paint that the model was originally painted with. When I was happy with the amount of dirt left on, I switched on the hair drier and blew off the remaining thinners to dry off the paint. I then rubbed the flat areas with a clean, dry cotton bud so that the matt brown took on the gentle sheen of a wagon that, although never cleaned, wasn't decrepit. Time taken? Five and a half minutes. The final act was to add some chalk writing on the side, done with a fine 00 brush, and more underframe gunge.

Photographed at Tyseley Works, this wagon is practically ex-works, and just like many models, it is too clean! It looks most unreal.

This 00 gauge A4 is a perfectly standard Hornby engine, unmodified apart from repainting. The paint is P100 BR Loco Green applied directly to the cleaned black plastic of the engine, as bought. Lining is H9 Tan and H21 Gloss Black. The only modification I had to do was cut back the boiler band behind the nameplate to get it to lie flat.

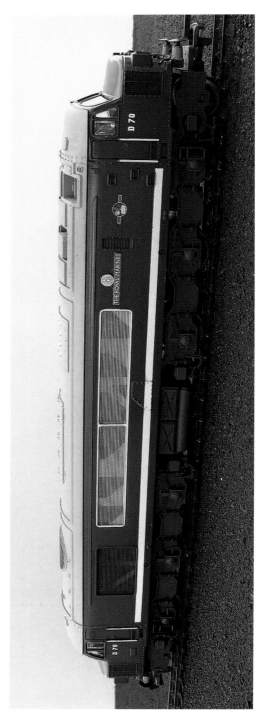

This is a dead basic Mainline Class 45, which came to me in BR blue. After preparation, the first paint was the grey stripe and body side vent sprayed without masking. Masks were cut to exact size and carefully positioned so that they were horizontal and straight. The next colour was the roof grey, again unmasked. This was masked before the green was sprayed. While the body was drying between coats, I painted the chassis in my usual mix of black and brown 'weathering'. Finally I ran some very dilute black into the louvres, dirty thinners really, to pick out the detail, and sprayed a similar mix onto the roof. It's not weathering as such but it removes the 'straight out of the box' look. Pity about the couplings.

CHAPTER NINE
READY-TO-RUN MODELS

The paints used on both Bachmann and Hornby models are cellulose based and are designed to key into the surface of the plastic by carefully managed softening and resetting, avoiding surface distortion. It follows that the paint is difficult to remove. The only effective method is by using a gentle softener, such as 'Superstrip' or equi-valent but this can take days and may still leave paint in corners and wells.

The lining (on flat areas) and other lettering and marks are all printed with ink using the 'Tampo' process. This uses soft silicone rubber printing heads to pick up the ink and place it precisely on the model. The use of a soft material allows the design to be printed over rivets and other small surface features. The boiler bands, being on a three-dimensional curved surface, cannot be printed, so these are sprayed with paint through a mask.

The ink can be removed readily with methylated spirit and a cotton bud. The boiler band paint, if it has to go, is best

The pair of Hale Fuels wagons are straightforward early Airfix wagons, both originally numbered 241. The one on the left has only had the wheels and couplings changed and the number altered by overpainting the figure '1'. The body of the wagon on the right was brushed over with very dilute matt black, which was then removed with a spirit-damp brush to leave traces on the surface and around the projections. The underframe was brushed with a black and brown mix from a palette so that the proportions of the colours varied. This wagon had its number altered by overpainting the '2'. This is five-minute 'weathering' and customising.

These are two early Mainline, now Bachmann, LMS period I coaches. In the time-honoured fashion, only a Brake Third and a Composite were issued. The coach on the right is the basic, unaltered composite. I altered the period of the BTK, on the left, by giving it the full panelled lining style in gold and black, and finished it with PC, now HMRS, Methfix insignia transfers and a gently weathered underframe. The roof is sprayed in basic H67, matt grey. Brass door handles and metal wheels complete the picture.

removed by scraping with a curved blade scalpel. If you are repainting with a different lining style, I would recommend removing the existing lining as its footprint will be visible through the new layer of paint.

The problem with plastic is that it is very soft and any mechanical methods used to remove paint from awkward areas may result in scratching the plastic. All in all, I would suggest leaving the existing paint in situ and painting over it. Check the paintwork closely as it is not unknown for there to be the odd speck of dust in it. Rub down imperfections extremely gently. Apart from this and a good clean with water-based products to remove dirt and finger marks, no other preparation is necessary. Any glazing that is glued in place will need to be masked, inside as well as out before spraying.

It is feasible to tone down the lining on steam locomotives by overlapping lines of body colour, as shown in the illustrations. If your pen skills are good enough, the orange/black/orange of GWR and BR can be converted to the correct sequence of colours by ruling in the extra green lines over the top of the black and orange.

The Tampo-printed lining can easily be removed with a cotton bud and Methylated Spirit.

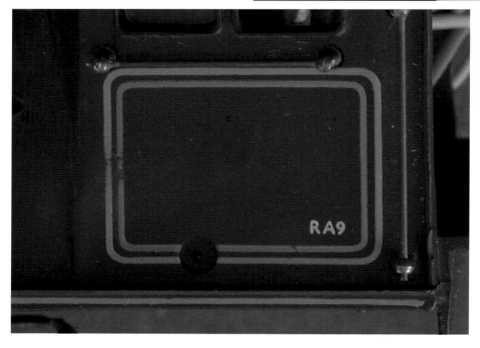

For a 'quick fix' on a Bachmann V2 it is possible to modify the existing lining. This secondhand one has part of the lining worn off.

Stage one is to rule over the red line with black paint to reduce its width. The corners, which have not been reduced in the photo, will need a bit of careful brush-work to reduce them to match the straight parts.

The corners have been reduced and the worn part painted over; H174 is a good match.

Next, the cream line is ruled in adjacent to the grey.

It is finished by filling in the corners of the cream. Although generally overscale, the lining is much improved. Now to tackle the valance!

The problem (1). At some point a previous owner had fixed onto the fire box an inappropriate safety valve. This had been removed and the area, including the adjacent cladding band, painted over in an inappropriate colour.

The area to be restored was cleaned with white spirit and then the depression in the paintwork was filled with neat paint, brushed in thickly. I used the nearest green in my collection for this. The illustration shows the result after 48 hours drying and the first rub down with 1200 grade wet and dry.

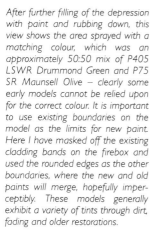

After further filling of the depression with paint and rubbing down, this view shows the area sprayed with a matching colour, which was an approximately 50:50 mix of P405 LSWR Drummond Green and P75 SR Maunsell Olive – clearly some early models cannot be relied upon for the correct colour. It is important to use existing boundaries on the model as the limits for new paint. Here I have masked off the existing cladding bands on the firebox and used the rounded edges as the other boundaries, where the new and old paints will merge, hopefully imperceptibly. These models generally exhibit a variety of tints through dirt, fading and older restorations.

CHAPTER TEN
RESTORATION

Although not my main line of business, I am occasionally commissioned to restore older models, eg. Bing, Märklin, Carette, Bassett-Lowke, Hornby, Leeds, etc, some of which are up to 100 years old. Restoration is a wide subject, possibly worth another book in itself, so I will give just a few pointers where it differs from the main terms of this work.

The essence of restoration, providing the model is not a complete wreck, is to preserve as much of the original paint as possible and not over restore. Collectors value the patina of age and can accept quite a large degree of distress if this is known to affect certain models.

The paint on early models is usually very thick, as if they were dipped in the paint. The paint would be matt but overlaid with a thick coat of gloss varnish. The varnish discolours with age, and also cracks, which makes it difficult to establish a good colour match. Conversely, other manufacturers used very thin paint without any form of primer, on to none too clean tinplate. A recipe for disaster.

Whether you regard these older models as possessing naïve charm or are grotesque parodies is a matter of choice, but they are worth A Lot Of Money. The model shown in the illustration is a Bing, for Bassett-Lowke, clockwork 2-4-2T that shares a wheel arrangement with the GWR 3600 Class, but little else. This model is worth about £2,000, so they are worth taking a great deal of care over.

Usually built from tinplate, they are prone to rust if not kept in a dry environment and it is this that may lead to the need to remove all the paint and start again. If a total repaint is required, you have the choice of a sympathetic replication of the original style or a 'scale' livery of the type I have covered. If you are looking to maximise value, then a repaint in the original style will be worth more.

Photograph your model in its original state, whether patch restoring or going for something more comprehensive. The photo is invaluable for showing which part is which colour (although not for matching colour) and for showing style and position of lining. Match the colours, keep your colour match samples and note down the recipe. These records become part of the provenance of the model and may be of interest to a future owner.

BASIC TECHNIQUES – FILLING HOLES AND GAPS
It is common for old models to have bits of paintwork missing, whether through knocks, rust or modification. The area concerned must be well cleaned and any rust dealt with either by means of a proprietary rust remover (from Halfords or equivalent) or careful fibre-glass brushing. Follow this with a rub with white spirit over the whole area that is to take new paint.

I find that the best way of filling is to use paint in layers. The usual body fillers are very sticky and tend to spread so that you end up rubbing down an area much greater than you started with, thus destroying more of the original finish than necessary. Paint can be controlled very precisely and wiped off if it ventures too far. You can also use this stage to get a close colour match. Once

the thickness of new paint appears to be above the surrounding original paint, and is fully cured, it can be gently rubbed down.

Start with no coarser than 1000 grade wet and dry. If working on a flat surface, stick the abrasive to a piece of thick card or Plastikard, so you don't rub a finger-shaped depression into the paint. Wet the abrasive with water and keep it wet. This will lubricate it and help stop it clogging. Apply only gentle pressure. Wipe the residues away regularly so that you can see how things are going. Any patches of new paint that remain glossy indicate that they are below the surface level and will need further filling. It can be a very slow job.

When you are happy that the job cannot be improved further, it is time for a gentle covering of paint to hide the repair. Ideally, this will be the whole area between natural boundaries on the model, eg, an edge or a colour change. This can mean that too much of the original paint is being covered, so painting a small patch will be better, although this will mean a high degree of colour matching. Use thin paint, gently covering the filled area and merging into the original.

BASIC TECHNIQUES – LINING
Early models were lined by young ladies using fine brushes. Some very early stuff was pretty crude but some of the last models by the original Bassett-Lowke company showed considerable skill, so that it is hard to tell whether a brush or pen was used.

The brushes were long bristled so that they held sufficient paint and also damped out any shakiness of the hand.

These are colours required to make the 'white' lining. H41 Ivory and H21 Gloss Black, P625 M&GN Golden Gorse and P75 SR Maunsell Dark Olive. The khaki colour is the result and amazingly it matched the existing. The mixing palette is a backing sheet from Fox Transfers, good glazed card, excellent for mixing paints on.

Left: After drying out for 24 hours, the result seems acceptable with no abrupt colour change. To match the other lining, the boiler bands need to be brushed on. To make this easier I have ruled guide lines on with a pen. While this paint is still wet it will hold the brush on line. A longer bristle brush is better for this sort of work. Right: The lines brushed on. To imitate the slight translucency of the original lining, I mixed a little linseed oil in with the paint.

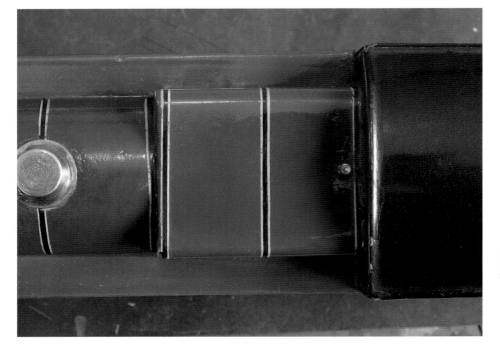

The black infill has been brushed in and the 'white' lines distressed slightly to match the other bands.

It will be necessary to replicate the style so it is essential that you have a photograph or another model to copy. If you are more confident with a pen than brush, draw yourself some guide lines to follow, with a ruling pen using the same paint. While the guide line is still wet, go over it with a brush. The tacky paint will guide the brush so that it should produce a decent straight line. (PRACTISE)

Lining paint can be some weird colours (note the khaki in the illustration) as a result of discoloration of the old varnish. It can also be translucent, visible at the edges. This can be replicated by reducing the density of the pigment by the addition of linseed oil or a slow-drying clear varnish. The exact proportion will have to be found by trial and error.

TIN PRINTED MODELS

Hornby, and to some extent Bassett-Lowke, used tin printed plate for their (usually lower cost) models. With these it is not possible to imitate the screen printing techniques used in their manufacture, just a close approximation. Paints must be applied carefully to avoid building up too great a thickness.

LETTERING

The lettering and numbering styles rarely conformed to a scale copy of the original so the use of today's transfers should be avoided if attempting a sympathetic restoration. The existing lettering must be carefully measured, traced and photographed if it is to be renewed. If the lettering is not too bad but the surrounding

paintwork needs renewing, it is possible to remove the paint but keep and mask off the lettering. I know, I've done it. I was given a Midland Railway tender to restore but the owner wanted to retain its number, 999, in its original state. I carefully cut the paint around the numbers with a new scalpel blade and then scraped the rest of the paint off without any trouble. After treating the rust and masking the numbers with Maskol, I sprayed the tender sides. After the Maskol was removed, just a minimal amount of brush filling was needed around the numbers to finish the job.

 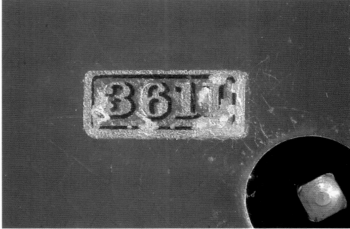

Left: *The second problem was that after years of use, the 'number plate' transfer is a little distressed, probably due to the key missing the hole.* Right: *Firstly the gold is replaced.*

Left: *And then the black with a fine brush.* Right: *And, finally, the red. This had to be let down with a little linseed oil as the original was translucent, allowing the backing silver to show through, to give a slightly metallic effect.*

PAINTING WOODEN BODIES

The main difference in painting wooden bodies is in the preparation. It is not a good idea to wet the wood for cleaning, so a good brush and blow to remove any dust, together with a wipe with a thinners damp cloth is all we can do.

I don't think it is worth doing any more surface preparation, such as rubbing down, at this stage, (except for gross blemishes which will need to be attended to). I find it better to get the primer on, let it dry thoroughly, then rub down.

The simplest way of priming is with an aerosol filler primer, applied evenly and not too thickly. If you are using the primer for the first time, apply some to some scrap for a test piece. Once dry, it must be rubbed down well. The point of rubbing down after priming is that unprimed wood can have surface fibres sticking out that will either not be fully removed by rubbing down, or that will be created by the process. After priming, the fibres are stiffened and will be snapped off by rubbing down and the rest will remain under the paint surface. If the wood grain is not to be visible in the completed model, then you must continue filling and rubbing down until the surface is smooth. The use of an automotive primer will speed this process up, as the drying time is so short.

Any bare areas will need to be re-primed thinly before top coats are applied. It is a good idea to prime both the inner and outer surfaces of the wood to prevent warping.

Because there is comparatively more surface preparation on a wooden model than a metal one, it is a good idea to fit any metal projecting parts, such as coach door handles and end steps, after surface preparation is complete.

Test your top coat out on the test piece and assess the results after 24 hours. The way paints are changing these days you never know what is in the can of primer. If all is OK, the top coats can be applied as for a metal-bodied model.

These models are to 16mm scale running on 32mm track, which I painted many years ago. They are built of plywood and hardwood strip, apart from the bogies and buffers. I painted them by first priming with Halfords red oxide primer, followed by lots of rubbing down with 280 grade paper and finishing with 1000 grade. The primer was topped up occasionally where it was rubbed thin. The maroon panels and white roofs were sprayed on but all the other colours were brushed. The timber framing and seats all received the two-coat graining procedure as described under 'Teak finish'. In this case it was wood painted to look like wood! I gave the second-class coach some lining to emphasise its higher status.

CHAPTER ELEVEN
FINISHING

TRANSFERS

Once all the paint is dry and we are satisfied that nothing can be improved, the finishing touches are numbering, lettering, plates and varnishing. Numbering and lettering are usually by transfer, of which there is a vast range available.

There are four types of transfers – waterslide, spirit fix, pressure fix and varnish. The latter type is rare and is generally associated with restoration of vintage models where replica transfers are available.

The largest range of transfers is of the waterslide type from Fox Transfers. These cover the most modern types back to the grouping of 1923, and a limited but growing range of earlier styles. HMRS Transfers cover the BR steam and early diesel periods, the Big Four and some pre-grouping companies, mainly LMS constituents plus NER and some GNR. These transfers are spirit fix (Methfix™) and pressure fix (Pressfix™). Some of the Methfix range has recently been discontinued due to lack of demand.

There are a number of other providers such as Guilplates and Dragon who can supply useful but smaller ranges for early railways.

SPIRIT FIX TRANSFERS

The best transfers are the spirit fix type, which are fixed with a dilute methylated spirit and then, when dry, the backing paper is washed off with water. The only range available is from HMRS Transfers (Methfix). On spirit fix transfers there is no halo of adhesive visible around the character. There seems to be a perceived difficulty amongst modellers I have spoken to about this type of transfer. I don't know why.

The method of use is simple. Score gently around the character to be transferred, lift a corner with a scalpel, then remove from the backing sheet with tweezers. Place on the model in position and then wet with a mix of three parts methylated spirit and one part water. The mix is fairly critical – too concentrated the paint will be attacked, too weak it will not activate the adhesive. Once wet, the tissue will become transparent, making the character more visible so that it can be moved to its

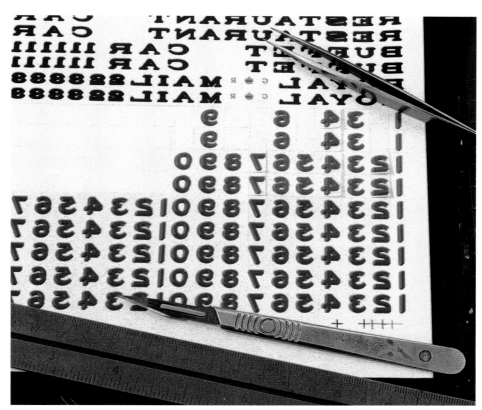

The corner of the Methfix transfer sheet with the relevant numbers scored and the corners lifted ready to be taken off with tweezers.

The transfers used for this engine are the HMRS Methfix LNER Green engine sheet. The letter transfers are relatively easy to position as they are already spaced out on the backing sheet. It is essential that the letters are centred and checked for horizontality, with dividers, while still dry. Once wetted with the dilute meths, it is best that they are not moved as they may get out of line while still under the backing paper. If that does happen, the paper will have to be lifted away (very carefully) in order to move the letters back into a straight line. They are extremely delicate, so make sure there is plenty of liquid to ease their movement but not enough for them to float off. The photograph shows a successful application with the paper mostly dried out.

Positioning the first number. I use two pairs of dividers for this, one set for the distance from the lining to the number – also used at the other end. The other is used to set the distance from the lower lining to the base of the number. The middle two numbers are set out at the same spacing as the letters on the front tender. The spacing is measured with the dividers and transferred to the rear tender. The orientation of the numbers must be checked continuously; luckily all these numbers have a horizontal component so that a visual check was easy.

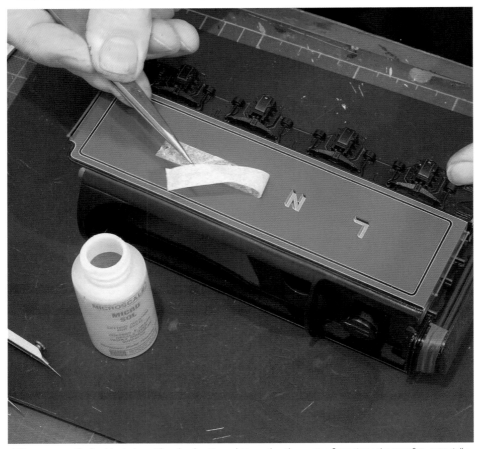

I like to remove the backing paper with a decal setting solution rather than water. Sometimes the transfers, especially the smaller ones, prefer to stick to the backing paper rather than the paint. The softening solution wets the paper better and reduces the adhesion.

final position, checking line with dividers and orientation with a square. Use a brush to remove excess liquid and press it gently on to the surface then leave it to dry, about ten minutes. After this period the backing tissue can he removed by soaking it in a decal softening solution, rather than water.

There are problems with smaller characters, such as power classifications, not sticking. This can be minimised by liberal application of the softening solution and very careful removal of the backing tissue. Alternatively, the backing tissue can be removed when the meths is applied, if it appears to be loose enough. Either way, brush some varnish over the transfer as soon as it is dry.

It is not recommended to remove the backing tissue from larger transfers at the meths stage, as the transfer will probably lift at the edges as the adhesive dries too fast.

When making up numbers or words, the backing tissue must be scored as close to the character as possible so that it does not prevent the characters being placed close together. Setting out numbers is very important as there is only a limited time for moving them around into line before the adhesive starts to set.

The transfers for whole words such as 'SOUTHERN' will need to be cut into two or three letter portions as the backing paper expands when wet, lifting some letters off the paint. When this happens, pressing them down again can push them out of line. Smaller portions are more manageable and can be lined up easily using the edges of the backing paper to get a straight line. Start from a properly set-out centre point and work outwards. This may seem a hassle but it is worth it.

PRESSURE FIX TRANSFERS

The most popular range of rub-down transfers is the Pressfix range by HMRS. The range duplicates the Methfix range. Most retailers only stock the Pressfix range, so to many people it is the only type of transfer available. As I discussed under transfer lining, the way to use it is to apply dilute meths to it when it is on the model but before it is stuck down. Numbers can be lined up more easily when you can see through the backing sheet.

I do have a problem with their thickness, and the halo of adhesive around the characters, so I rarely use Pressfix.

WATERSLIDE TRANSFERS

The third type of transfer is the waterslide type, which is easily the most popular for most modellers. This is due to the superb range available from Fox Transfers, which is now being expanded back in time to cover more of the steam era. In these transfers the adhesive is printed in the same footprint as the character, so the glossy backing of previous days is no longer a problem for single characters like 'LMS'. It still remains though for words such as 'SOUTHERN' or 'GREAT WESTERN'.

The Fox transfers for the BR emblems are excellent, especially the post-1956 ferret-and-dartboard where the details of the crown are visible, far better in my opinion, than the HMRS equivalent.

Fixing them is quite simple. Score right through the backing sheet, dip in water and after about 30 seconds the character can be slid off into position. Remove excess water before this or the transfer will float on top of a bubble of water, losing its adhesive into

This is a rare beast. A Metropolitan Railway Class H 4-4-4T, which became LNER Class H2. The model is to 0 gauge, built by Mike Edge. This was one of my early jobs which, apart from the company name, was reasonably straightforward. The lettering is in gold Letraset with added shading. There is another number on the rear of the bunker, which, I think, was the first hand-painted number that I had done.

This Campbelltown & Macrihanish Railway 0-6-2T in 009 is the Backwoods Miniatures kit, built by Mike Edge. This, again, is a railway whose livery is difficult to research. Reportedly based on the contemporary North British livery (whose 'bronze green' is as difficult as any to define), there are few photographs that show the disposition of the lining in any detail. I managed to find a photograph on the Internet, that I could enhance to get most of the detail, but no colours, of course. This is a model I painted some time ago and I have to admit to cheating on the lettering, which is Letraset with added blocking and shading.

solution. Gently press the transfer down to expel any air that may be trapped, then leave to dry out completely.

You may encounter problems when fixing transfers to matt-painted freight wagons. This manifests itself as a misty area behind the backing varnish of the transfer. It is caused by trapped air within the surface of the matt paint. The only solution, once the transfer is on, is to paint around the letters with the original body paint. If your paint came out of an aerosol can, all you can do is weep. The areas that are to take transfers must be smooth gloss so that all air can be squeezed out. Final matting can be done with the varnish.

VARNISH FIX TRANSFERS

These are an old type of transfer where the image is printed in reverse onto tissue without adhesive. In use, the back of the transfer is coated in varnish (or the area on the model can be coated instead) and the transfer placed in position and very gently teased into position and smoothed out. It is then left for 24 hours, the backing tissue wetted and pulled off.

The use these days tends to be limited to replica manufacturers' trade marks on older models, generally Hornby 0 gauge and Bassett-Lowke.

GENERAL

Take time with transfers. I know numbers were not always straight on the prototype but it looks bad on the model. Check where emblems and initials were placed in relation to rivets and beading – they were not always central to the panel.

There will be water and adhesive staining adjacent to waterslide and Methfix transfers. This can be removed by wiping with a water-damp cloth.

It is important to check from photographs the size of letters and numbers used on your prototype. The LNER and GWR were very consistent in this respect but the Southern and LMS were not. The Southern used many sizes of number during the Maunsell period and it is not always obvious which size should be used, so proportioning from a photograph will be necessary.

The LMS could never quite decide what its 'corporate image' should be. Full details of the variations can be found in Volume I of the *Locomotives of the LMS* by Essery and Jenkinson.

During the BR period there was much variation in positioning numbers, power classifications and route availability numbers. For example, of the three regions that used the power classification system, there were three different ways of indicating a mixed traffic locomotive. The LMR used just a number (4). The SR used both P and F (4P4F) and the ScR used MT (4MT) for tender engines and MTT for tank engines.

This is a Newbold Models LBSC Class 13 kit in 0 gauge, built by Peter Dobson. It is a locomotive of simple lines and well balanced, in an attractive livery. Transfers are by Methfix. Quite graceful really, what more can I say?

NAME AND NUMBER PLATES

These should be fixed before the model is varnished, as the varnish will help prevent the polished brass tarnishing.

Pay a little attention to the edges of the plates, especially prominent name plates. Most 4mm scale plates come ready etched to shape, so all you need to do is gently file off the etching cusp with a very fine file (a curved file for concave edges). Take care with the filing as these plates are very thin and can bend and crease easily.

The plates provided by Guilplates, which are the most popular in O gauge, come fretted out so need a little more attention. There is no etching cusp, of course, but they will have been cut out slightly proud of the true edge and will need filing back. Finish the edges with fine emery.

Name and number plates often need an extra coat of paint to improve on the thin factory finish. Brush or spray as you wish but do not bother to keep the paint off the characters. When the plate is dry, gently rub the face onto a sheet of fine emery to remove the paint from the face of the characters.

A large number of GWR engines had cast-iron number plates, a fact happily ignored by most modellers. These should have the numbers picked out in cream paint, fiddly but authentic. Likewise, BR smokebox numbers should be painted white (or off white) and not left as brass or nickel silver.

The back of the plates must be cleaned of any adhesive, etching resist and tarnish and then roughened up a little with the tip of a scribe, to give a bit of key for the adhesive. I always stick plates on with Evo-stik Impact adhesive. I apply the glue with the tip of a cocktail stick along the centre of the plate and then, with tweezers, place it very carefully in position, check its alignment, tweak if necessary and then press it down. If the glue is placed too near the edge, there is a danger that it might leak out during the adjustment stage. You do not need to apply the glue to both surfaces.

Stand-up nameplates on splashers will need something to stick to. If the kit did not provide brackets, you will, of course, have made them up and soldered them on

during construction? If not, make a couple from scrap brass and solder (to an unpainted plate) or super glue (to a painted plate) on the back.

The backing plate of GWR names will need to be painted; you would do this when painting the rest of the engine. If the plate comes ready painted, check that the green matches the one you have used or, if necessary, change it to black for the early BR period. Any lining on the number plates is best done before they are detached from the backing card. If lining the name backing plate, you need to be aware that the top and bottom curves may not share the centre point. If using normal compasses stick the plates to a piece of plastic card and find the upper and lower radii with dividers. If using offset compasses, make sure that the edges are absolutely true, then put in the lower line from the bottom edge and the upper line from the top edge of the name plate. The remaining two short edges are best done with offset compasses or fine brush work.

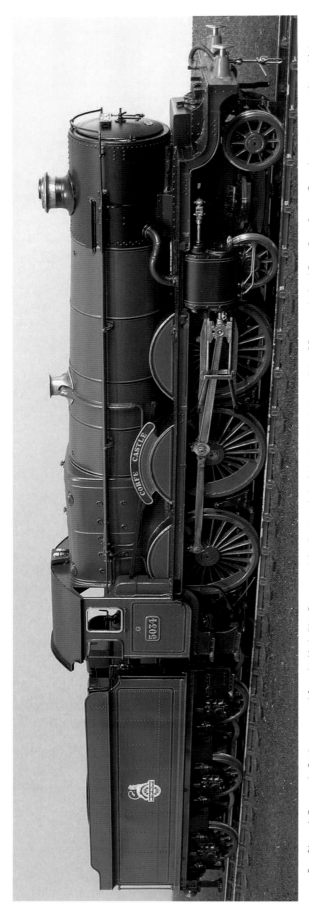

Pete Silvester's 7mm scale Castle constructed from the Mitchell kit. Pete painted the chassis and wheels. I painted the body in cellulose BR green, aka Land Rover Deep Bronze Green. I gave it a very gentle varnish in Ronseal Gloss with just a little matting agent added.

I built this O gauge Patriot for myself. I built it from the Gladiator kit but added a few extra details, particularly on the front of the tender, which is quite visible. The body was painted in cellulose Deep Bronze Green. It is seen here in nearly ex-works condition. They were actually turned out like this sometimes, with the topside repainted but the frames and wheels untouched. This is now ready to be weathered. It has not been varnished.

VARNISHING

As it approaches completion, the model will have a variety of surface finishes from the various types of paint used. These will be unified by a coat of varnish and the depth of colour will be enhanced. I always use Ronseal polyurethane (not the quick-drying variety) which is available in gloss, satin or matt finishes, but I have never used the matt. I have found that the satin has become unreliable as the matting agent tends to give a coarse glint to the surface under artificial lighting so I now use the gloss with a little PQ14 Matting Agent added. It's a situation where a degree of experimentation is required as it is not an exact science. I find that enough matting agent to cover the end of a small screwdriver (3mm wide blade), is sufficient when mixed in with an airbrush cupful of diluted varnish. I spray on the lightest of coats of very dilute varnish, at a pressure of about 40 psi, which gives a beautiful even finish. The use of varnish gives some protection to the transfers. A single drop of black in the varnish will dull down bright transfers and give the engine a 'couple of days in traffic' look.

The spraying distance will affect the surface finish. Spraying from afar with lots of air will produce a more matt finish.

If you have used cellulose paints, a cellulose gloss lacquer can be sprayed on very thinly with a high air:paint ratio to give a silky finish, without affecting enamel lining paints. The idea behind this is that the thinners will have evaporated away before hitting the model so that any enamels will be unaffected.

The coat of varnish will be the last thing to land on your ex-works engine. You will have invested a lot of time in putting on a smooth coat of primer, getting the paint finish right, the lining right and the various transfers straight and square, so do not cock it up on this, the last stage.

A friend of mine, who will be shocked and horrified to read this, once messed up his varnish (I think a thumb print was involved). Now don't laugh at this, but he started to rub down the varnish while it was still tacky, with disastrous results. Needless to say, it was a strip down to bare metal and start again. Luckily, it was only a side tank so the rest of the paintwork on the engine could be saved.

It is a good idea to let the model stand for a week before varnishing. Before you reach for the varnish, some more preparation is required. During lining and fixing transfers, you will probably have touched the model with bare hands so it will need a gentle wash. A wipe over areas that you have touched will be sufficient, it won't all need to be cleaned. Use a paper towel just damp with white spirit or with dilute detergent.

If anything untoward happens at the varnish stage, you have a choice of two solutions. As I mentioned in the section on enamel spraying, a discrete area can be cleaned of varnish with a spirit-damp paper towel or cotton bud, while it is still fresh. If the varnish is touch dry but still young, it may be possible to lift it with a rub from a spirit-damp cotton bud. In all other cases the varnish should be allowed to dry and then be rubbed down with fine emery.

Acrylic and cellulose varnishes (lacquers) can only be removed by rubbing down.

If you intend to weather the engine, there is no real need to varnish it; after all, the real ones left the works bright and shiny, even the lowliest shunter, before they became weathered.

Finally, put a spot of matt paint on those surfaces that are obviously matt – hoses and the cab and tender floors.

Having completed the painting, the final stage is to give it the finish you require and protect any transfers – gloss Ronseal with added matting agent, if required, or a cellulose lacquer, carefully applied.

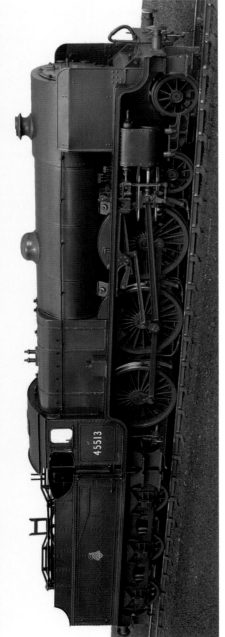

45513 again after weathering. I copied a photo of a shiny but dirty engine and followed the Martyn Welch method to get the finish I wanted. The chassis and wheels were painted in a gunge colour to start with, then various rusty highlights were added. Not often seen, in fact I don't recall ever seeing on a model, is the black outline to the BR cab numbers. As it is mine, I ruled them in adjacent to the transfer numbers.

The 'half' splasher was lined on its vertical edge. The Western Region differed.

CHAPTER TWELVE
WEATHERING

Now that we have an ex works engine or coach, do we want to go a stage further and weather it? It is entirely up to you, it's your model. If you do wish to, then I would fully recommend Martyn Welch's book *The Art of Weathering* published by Wild Swan.

Notwithstanding the statements in Martyn's book, it does not matter whether you use enamel, acrylic or cellulose as your base coat. With cellulose and acrylic you can start weathering within the hour, but, providing you wait a couple of days, enamel is quite safe provided you have used gloss paint, which will dry nice and hard.

I don't intend to spend too much time on weathering techniques as it is not the focus of the book, but for a quick fix, on an engine that may never have been cleaned in real life, gently spray very dilute matt or satin black, with a hint of dark grey added,

over the superstructure to replicate soot that has landed on it, with more landing on the horizontal surfaces than the rest. Below the running plate, add a little brown to the mix (eg. Brick Red, H70), to imitate brake dust. Rusty areas like the ashpan and behind step plates can receive a little Matt Leather (H62) either sprayed or dry brushed. That's it. Minimal weathering. Don't overdo it.

For something a little more sophisticated, for a non-black engine, spray Gloss Black enamel, thinly over the superstructure, then take most of it off after a couple of hours. This can be done with cotton buds just damp with white spirit (preferably on the smooth areas as cotton buds are apt to leave wisps of cotton on any projection). Otherwise use a spirit-damp paint brush or a lint-free cloth. The idea is to leave a deposit around projections, and streaks cir-

cumferentially around the boiler, as if the cleaner has had a go but it was too much for him.

Take care to clean under the boiler side hand rails as the cleaners could easily reach these areas. A line of dirt behind the rail is not prototypical.

Study a photo of the real thing. This stage can be repeated to increase the amount of dirt left after cleaning.

Stage two is a gentle blow over with H Metalcote Gun Metal. Just a hint, again very dilute. This will dry almost instantly and can be polished up to represent the glint that comes off the edges of even dirty vehicles. Finally, add a layer of soot, as described above.

Diesel weathering follows broadly the same pattern as steam locomotives, but there is the added advantage that the

The London Midland Region green engines carried the most 'correct' form of the BR livery from its inception. The splasher face is lined only along the top curve in black/green/orange (the Western Region differed). The valance edge is black with the orange line spaced away from it (the Western Region differed). Dimensions did vary, depending on the depth of the valance.

An engine that is dirty but looked after and has the 'shiny dirty' look. The model is to 7mm scale, built from the North Star kit by Greg Goodman. After the paint had dried for a week, I used the techniques described in the Weathering section to produce the effect – a mist coat of black, which was then removed with a spirit-damp cotton bud so that the 'dirt' collected around the projections. The bud was flattened in a vice to get it under the hand rails. All the brass and copper work was brushed over with very dilute gloss black paint so that it gathered in the corners, emphasising the contours and imparting a dull sheen. The chassis and flat parts of the superstructure received various sprayed and dry-brushed colours from the Martyn Welch palette.

working locomotives exist on the real railways so that by observing and photographing them you at least have something to copy. There are more colour photographs of the green and blue period diesels in various publications, some of which show quite filthy machines. The poor steam-period modeller has to rely on colour photos of the late BR period, hardly typical of the long history of steam.

Modern diesels tend to be quite clean machines – they are operating in a much cleaner environment and their appearance is a marketing statement for their owners. Weathering a model of these machines would be restricted to underframe dirt, exhaust staining of the roof and, of course, dead flies on the yellow panels.

For coaches, the overall 'dirt' spray would be satin rather than gloss as coaches were cleaned with soapy water rather than oily rags. The underframes and bogies can generally be painted in a uniform gunge colour. Weathering a panelled coach adds a lot of character to it. Just be gentle, you don't want to hide all that lining!

Many pregrouping railways used white lead on the roof of coaches to waterproof the canvas covering. It was purely functional, not decorative, so it was allowed to get dirty, which it did within seconds of entering traffic. Even if you don't weather the sides of your coaches, it looks better if the roofs have a wisp of dirt on them.

I have said above that wagons should be weathered, but as this area is such a complex subject, given the battering and lack of care, I can only refer you to Martyn Welch's book for the techniques required.

This is another West Country built by John Edwards, this time from the Martin Finney kit. The chassis has been weathered by John but the superstructure is ex-works. The BR livery is easier to do than the Southern as the black infill between the orange lines is more forgiving than the yellow.
Photo by JOHN EDWARDS

I drew the black edging around the cabside numbers. This feature is rarely seen on a model.

CONCLUSION

I hope that painting and lining is no longer such a dark and magic art. I have explained the techniques but I cannot give you practice and patience. Practice is the key. The best equipment you can afford is a close second. But neither is any good without a photograph of the prototype.

APPENDIX

Fig. 11 – SCALE WIDTHS OF LINING IN MILLIMETRES

Scale	N/2mm 150	TT/3mm 100	00/4mm 76	S 64	0/7mm 43.5	1/10mm 32	G 22.5	3.5" 16	5" 12
Inches									
1/8	0.02	0.03	0.04	0.05	0.07	0.10	0.14	0.20	0.26
1/4	0.04	0.06	0.08	0.10	0.15	0.20	0.28	0.40	0.53
3/8	0.06	0.10	0.13	0.15	0.22	0.30	0.42	0.60	0.79
1/2	0.08	0.13	0.17	0.20	0.29	0.40	0.56	0.79	1.06
5/8	0.11	0.16	0.21	0.25	0.36	0.50	0.71	0.99	1.32
3/4	0.13	0.19	0.25	0.30	0.44	0.60	0.85	1.19	1.59
7/8	0.15	0.22	0.29	0.35	0.51	0.69	0.99	1.39	1.85
1	0.17	0.25	0.33	0.40	0.58	0.79	1.13	1.59	2.12
2	0.34	0.51	0.67	0.79	1.17	1.59	2.26	3.18	4.23
3	0.51	0.76	1.00	1.19	1.75	2.38	3.39	4.76	6.35
4	0.68	1.02	1.34	1.59	2.34	3.18	4.52	6.35	8.47
5	0.85	1.27	1.67	1.98	2.92	3.97	5.64	7.94	10.58
6	1.02	1.52	2.01	2.38	3.50	4.76	6.77	9.53	12.70

Fig. 12 – BRITISH RAILWAYS GREEN LOCOMOTIVE LINING

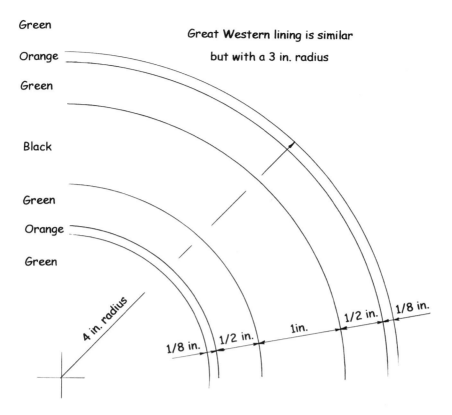

Fig. 13 – BRITISH RAILWAYS AND LNWR BLACK LOCOMOTIVE LINING

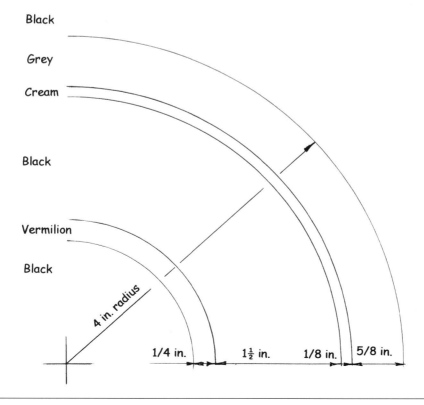

SUPPLIERS

Phoenix Precision Paints Ltd
Paints – enamel & acrylic
PO Box 8238, CHELMSFORD, CM1 7WY
01268 730549
www.phoenix-paints.co.uk

Railmatch Paints
Paints – acrylic
Howes Models Ltd, 12, Banbury Road, KIDLINGTON,
OX5 2BT
01865 848000
www.howesmodels.co.uk

Comet Models
Paints – cellulose
105, Mossfield Road, KING'S HEATH, B14 7JE
05602 602 188
www.cometmodels.co.uk

Chris Wesson
Paints – cellulose
11 Hestia Close, ROMSEY, SO51 8PA
01794 511535
http://website.lineone.net/~cbwesson

CPL Products
Transfers, scale rules
4 The Glade, NEWBURY, RG14 7AT
01635 44001

ModelocoMecca
Paints – cellulose
PO Box 4389, DUDLEY, DY1 9AF
01902 650077
www.modelloco-mecca.com

Fox Transfers
Transfers and paints
138 Main Street, MARKFIELD, LE67 9UX
01530 245958
www.fox-transfers.co.uk

HMRS Transfers
Methfix & Pressfix Transfers
8 Gilpin Green, HARPENDEN, AL5 5NR

Hannants
XtraDecal transfer paper
Harbour Road, Oulton Broad, LOWESTOFT, NR32 3LZ
01502 517444
www.hannants.co.uk

247 Developments
Name & number plates
18 Glyn Close, BARWELL, LE9 8GL
01455 843212
errolsurnam@247developments.freeserve.co.uk

Model Master
Name & number plates
Transfers
PO Box 8560, TROON, Scotland, KA10 6WX
01292 314458
www.modelmasterdecals.com

CGW
Name & number plates
Plas Cadfor, LLWYNGWRIL, LL37 2LA
01483 848 101
www.internationalmodels.net

Severn Mill Nameplates
Name & number plates
47 High Street, WALCOTT, LN4 3SW
01526 860983
www.severnmillnameplates.co.uk

Guilplates
Name & number plates
Transfers
32, Wodeland Avenue, GUILDFORD, GU2 4JZ
01483 565980
guilplat@globalnet.co.uk

Dragon Models
Transfers
9 Kingsley Close, PENARTH, CF64 5UW
02920 531246
chrisbasten@dragonmodels.fsnet.co.uk

P P Scene
Haff drawing instruments
68 High Street, CHISELHURST, BR7 5BL
020 8467 7490

Haff
Precision drawing instruments
Gebrüder Haff GmbH
Tiroler Strasse 5, D-87459 PFRONTEN
Germany
+49-8363-91220
www.Haff.com

Squires
Paints, Airbrushes
Magnifiers
100, London Road, BOGNOR REGIS,
PO21 1DD
01243 842424

Machine Mart
Air tools
Stores nationwide
0870 770 7840
www.machinemart.co.uk

Widespread Solutions Ltd
Spray booths
Unit 1 Levens Hall Park, Lund Lane,
Killinghall, HARROGATE, HG2 3BG
01423 522836
www.widespreadsolutions.co.uk

The Airbrush Co
Airbrushes & spray guns
Unit 7, Marlborough Road, Lancing Business Park,
LANCING, BN15 8UF
08700 660 445
http://airbrushes.com

Activity Media
Painting & Lining DVD
Ian Rathbone + Tony Wright
7 Conway Drive
FLITWICK, Beds, MK45 1DE
01525 759047
www.activitymedia.co.uk

Missenden Modellers' Weekend
Construction and painting courses
C J Langdon, 13 Lodge End, RADLETT,
Herts, WD7 7EB
01923 854684
www.missendenrailwaymodellers.org.uk

Hobby Holidays
Construction and painting courses
Phil & Jo Atkinson, The Spinney, Low Street, Beckingham,
DONCASTER, DN10 4PW
01427 848979
www.hobbyholidays.co.uk

> During the period of writing this book, the situation in regard to suppliers and products has changed continually, resulting in errors creeping into the text. Railmatch Paints continue to sell enamel paints and the HMRS continues to market its full range of transfers.